Asperger's Syndrome

Asperger's Syndrome

A GUIDE TO HELPING YOUR CHILD THRIVE AT HOME AND AT SCHOOL

Melinda Docter, Ed.D.
and
Syed Naqvi, M.D.

WILEY

John Wiley & Sons, Inc.

Published by John Wiley & Sons, Inc., Hoboken, New Jersey
Published simultaneously in Canada

For general information about our other products and services, please contact our Customer Care Department within the United States at (800) 762-2974, outside the United States at (317) 572-3993 or fax (317) 572-4002.

Wiley also publishes its books in a variety of electronic formats. Some content that appears in print may not be available in electronic books. For more information about Wiley products, visit our web site at www.wiley.com.

Library of Congress Cataloging-in-Publication Data:

Docter, Melinda.
    Asperger's syndrome : a guide to helping your child thrive at home and at school / Melinda Docter and Syed Naqvi.
        p.   cm.
    Includes bibliographical references and index.
    ISBN 978-0-470-14014-7 (pbk.); ISBN 978-0-470-63042-6 (ebk);
    ISBN 978-0-470-63072-3 (ebk); ISBN 978-0-470-63074-7 (ebk)
    1. Asperger's syndrome in children—Popular works.   I. Naqvi, Syed, M.D.   II. Title.
    RJ506.A9.D63   2010
    618.92'858832—dc22

                                                                          2010013181

Printed in the United States of America

10 9 8 7 6 5 4 3 2 1

Contents

Introduction

Asperger's syndrome is defined as a lack of effective reciprocity in verbal and nonverbal social interaction and of the ability to put yourself in someone else's shoes. The description of the higher-functioning characteristics of this disorder has changed little from that given in the classic paper by Austrian pediatrician Hans Asperger in 1943.

Recent advances in biology, neuroimaging, clinical research, and medication intervention (psychopharmacology) have had an enormous impact on quality of life and long-term outcomes for individuals with Asperger's syndrome and their parents or other caregivers.

At present, the incidence of Asperger's syndrome, which is a higher-functioning form of autism, is found in one in one hundred and ten children—which represents a 57 percent increase since 2002—and it occurs in boys four times as often as it occurs in girls. Asperger's syndrome frequently manifests in social disturbances in day-to-day living, both at home and at school. Many of the afflicted children have issues of sensory sensitivity with touch, smell, taste, and sound that go way beyond what can be considered normal. Because of the significant disruption that this causes in their daily lives, these children are not able to participate in developmentally typical or normal activities, such as school events, public outings, and playdates.

An innate difficulty in understanding another person's state of mind or perception of a situation is a hallmark of this disorder, and it causes significant disruption in peer interactions and school functioning. Comorbidity—which means having additional psychiatric and/or medical problems, such as attention or focus issues, anxiety, obsessions or compulsions, and mood instability—compounds the complexity of the primary diagnosis.

Enormous progress in understanding the syndrome, combined with early intervention and structured life at school and home, has had a significant impact on the long-term growth and prognosis of these children. Many now have a viable plan of self-care and are much more integrated into the larger society, which means being able to hold a job, live independently, and have close and fulfilling personal relationships.

These are exciting times in the field of Asperger's syndrome. Besides the recent advances in biology and neuroimaging, the Food and Drug Administration (FDA) approved the drugs risperidone in 2006 and aripiprazole in 2008 for irritability and aggression in children five to sixteen years old with autism. This has pushed many of us to reevaluate our treatment approaches for the higher-functioning children in the domain of Asperger's syndrome children. This book will reflect these advances.

The progress in dealing with this disease goes beyond biological interventions. The issues of sensory overload and behavioral abnormalities have been shown to respond favorably to behavior modification and sensory integration techniques. These supports are provided by schools and clinic-based occupational therapists. Speech and language therapy works on practical language and conversation skills, both receptive and expressive. Adaptive physical education provides support for modified physical activity and balance issues. Physical therapy enhances gross motor skills, range-of-motion capacities, and balance. Behaviorist psychology techniques in the home and in school teach appropriate social behavior, anger management, coping skills, and conflict resolution. Clinical studies have validated the importance of these interventions in the psychological and social lives of individuals with Asperger's syndrome. This book will give an overview based on personal professional experiences of these developments.

Finally, the spiritual lives of these individuals should not be ignored. We will try to reflect what is reasonable and amenable for change and what is not in the life journey of these individuals. Parents and other caregivers need to be aware that in their zeal to make a difference, the first maxim is to do no harm. This is difficult and at times impossible to accept, due to an often subjective interpretation of what is meant by *harm*.

The United States has a unique perspective on how to foster independence. At the age of eighteen, the parental cord is cut as many students move away from home and into college dorms. Children with Asperger's syndrome need to do this, too, but sometimes they are kept at home much longer than they should be. A typical thirteen- or fourteen-year-old is pushing away, and the parents are often trying to allow them to do so.

In Asperger's syndrome, however, this doesn't happen. The child does not push away, and the mother or father always comes to the rescue. Children with Asperger's syndrome should be allowed to fall. They shouldn't be allowed to break their legs, but they should be allowed to skin their knees and learn from the experience. Independence should be a goal. The social milieu must take over from the parents, but many parents disagree with us on this. Parents need to have a strategic plan to assist their children in becoming independent. We hope that this book serves as a guide to parents in easing the transition into adult independence, whatever that may mean for each child.

This book is meant to serve as a general guide to the biological, psychological, social, and spiritual developments in the management of children with Asperger's syndrome. It explores several areas of challenge for these children. Each chapter includes a medical perspective and a section on medical intervention written by Syed Naqvi, a medical doctor, as well as a home-to-school perspective and intervention written by Melinda Docter, a doctor of education and a parent of a child previously diagnosed with Asperger's syndrome. Some chapters will be written by only one author, depending on the subject matter.

We feel privileged to share the trials and tribulations and the joy in the lives of individuals who suffer from Asperger's syndrome. A decade of work in this field and our participation in the lives of these individuals has convinced us that there is always hope, and with that hope comes a great understanding of the human condition.

1

A Mother's Longing to Understand Her Son

I (Melinda) am not a psychiatrist or a psychologist. I am the mother of two children and an educator and a researcher in the field of people with disabilities. One of my children, my son, has received a diagnosis of Asperger's syndrome. The other child, my daughter, is relatively fine; however, she has my genetic predisposition for anxiety and depression.

My son has spent the first ten years of his life hoping that the world around him would understand him and that he would understand it. Sometimes this happens, and sometimes it does not.

When it does not, his world is filled with misunderstanding, misinterpretation, social blunders, depression, anxiety, and fear. He is depressed about today and afraid for tomorrow. His obsessions take over, and he is unable to use his skills to engage in typical daily activities.

When life is at its best, he is happy, relatively well-adjusted, interactive, and social. His world is filled with activities, friends, playdates, and sleepovers. During those times, he has somehow been given the opportunity to grow within a safe environment and has succeeded. He looks forward to tomorrow and to growing up. Most important, he lives with hope and self-confidence.

My life as Zachary's mother has been the life of an interpreter. It is a role that has proved to be very beneficial for Zachary in understanding the world around him and feeling confident enough to take risks. I learned the job requirements from Zachary, for he is the only one who can truly explain what kind of help he needs and how he needs it. It is through his perceptions of his environment, his use of language, his nonverbal communication, and his feelings about himself and others that my husband and I have learned how to provide instruction, intervention, support, and encouragement.

Our Story

After thirty-seven hours of labor, I gave birth to Zachary. He had a very short umbilical cord. His Apgar score was normal, and he came home with me after a day and a half. Life was not what I expected, however. Zachary screamed for hours at a time. He wanted to eat every hour and a half and was never satisfied. The more we tried to comfort him, the more agitated he became and the more anxious we became. He awakened every forty-five minutes during the night and screamed until exhaustion took over and another forty-five minutes had passed. He had nursing problems as well as gastrointestinal problems, and we were tired.

This went on for three months. Then we began to see a small glimmer of hope that we could begin to enjoy our first child. He began to smile, be content for short periods, and respond to visual stimuli such as toys and books. However, stroller rides were out of the question, car rides were a nightmare, and the sleep issue was still all-consuming. Repeated trips to the pediatrician proved useless; we did not understand our son any more than we did when he first came home from the hospital.

When Zachary was four months old, we began Gymboree classes, because that's what new parents did. Zachary was barely able to tolerate the noise, the visual stimuli, and the constant motion. He was cranky and agitated, and we were nervous. We quit after a month. It was about then that I realized he could not tolerate the sounds of other infants screaming. That made trips to the mall, the doctor's office, the market, and the park extremely difficult and anxiety-producing for all of us.

Zachary's physical development and speech development were within the normal range. He sat up, crawled, stood, and walked all within the normative developmental standards. Socially, however, Zachary was behind. When he was nine months old, we decided to attempt Gymboree again. Infants at that age do not appear to have any frame of reference for personal space and personal boundaries. I watched infants of this age crawl all over one another as if they were part of the Gymboree equipment. The infants who were being crawled over paid little or no attention to the additional little person invading their space.

Then I watched my son. He had determined, at nine months, that if there was personal space to be had, he would have it. As he watched the other infants crawling toward him, he would scream or put his hand out as if to say, "You're too close." He refused to stay in the circle and was not the least bit interested in anything that the other Gymboree members were doing. I left Gymboree knowing that something was not quite right. This was the beginning of several situations like that, before I actually knew *what* was not quite right.

Zachary's preschool experience began when he was two and a half years old, preceded by Mommy and Me classes. Zachary was fearful, anxious, and not the slightest bit interested in LEGOs, circle time, group songs, or interactive play. As the other children proceeded through the normative developmental path—parallel play, interactive play, imaginative play, sharing, and conversations with appropriate topic maintenance—Zachary did not. He played, but not with toys. He was interactive, but only with adults. He was imaginative, but none of his peers wanted to re-create the drapes at the dentist's office or do any of the other things that filled his imagination. He had conversations, but only if he chose the topic and the recipient was just the listener.

Zachary was in trouble. We could see it, and we did everything we could to help him. We made playdates, kept him on topic, monitored his conversations, and made several attempts to interest him in "normal" activities. However, Zachary's unusual interests, his extreme anxiety in new situations, and his commitment to routine kept him from making much progress.

He did not have any innate coping skills. Everything had to be taught to him, and to do this we began a game of predicting everything: who would be at the birthday party, which cousin might not play with him at Grandma's house, what he should do if someone was on the swing that he wanted, how he should respond when someone said hello, what would happen if he threw a fit in the mall, who would pick him up from school—any and every change in his normal routine, and on and on. Most of our conversations with Zachary were based on predictions, and although it was a very unusual way to interact with a three-year-old, it greatly reduced his anxiety and increased his ability to feel comfortable and take risks.

When Zachary was three and a half, the director of the pre-school informed me that he was not developing socially in the manner that she had grown to expect from children. I screamed back at her that "there is such a thing as parallel play, you know" and then went to buy my first book on autism. The book described a child with autism as one who did not show affection, who did not speak, and who rocked back and forth. I breathed a sigh of relief and put the book back on the shelf.

I asked Zachary why he didn't play with any of the children in his class. My three-year-old answered, "Sometimes I play with them; sometimes I don't. It's my choice, Mommy." Who was I to say that it wasn't? Unfortunately, my instincts were telling me that it wasn't always a choice. Maybe, just maybe, it was because he didn't have the skills to play with other children.

Zachary now had a baby sister who was nine months old. We had waited for his jealous reaction to a new sibling, for him to interact with her, take care of her, and show her off. None of it happened. We laughed at the idea that Zachary was so jealous that he blocked her completely from his reality. We laughed a year later when he said, "I'm going to play my guitar, Mommy, but I'll be quiet, because someone is sleeping. What's her name?" We even laughed when his sister pulled a chair over on top of herself and was crying and Zachary responded by asking us to take her out of the room because she was making too much noise. None of this was funny. In actuality, these were all symptoms, but we wouldn't know that for another two years.

As Zachary progressed through preschool, he mildly improved in his social interactions and in his ability to cope with new situations. However, the perseverative nature of his interests made it extremely difficult for him to make friends. No other four-year-olds wanted to build printing presses with wooden blocks, study street signs, or watch fountains and windmills for hours on end. No other four-year-olds loved wallets, tape, or offices. Nor could they re-create their interests by drawing in perspective. No one else had the same interests that Zachary had, but he didn't care. He was perfectly content to pursue his interests alone and not make friends.

You would think that with Zachary's need for routine and structure, he would have loved kindergarten, but he did not. He found it boring, unstimulating, and full of rules that made no sense to him. Why couldn't you move to the next center if you were done with an activity? Why couldn't you draw your current obsession if you didn't like what was assigned? Why did you have to share the computer when it was your turn?

Kindergarten was neither heartbreaking nor exhilarating for any of us, however. It was first grade that was the turning point.

I was teaching third grade at Zachary's elementary school the year he started first grade. Every day I would go home for lunch, and every day I would drive back to see Zachary wandering aimlessly around the playground by himself or sitting on a bench by himself watching the other children. Once in a while I would catch a glimpse of him running with the other children, and for a split second my mind would be put at ease because I would think, "He's okay, he's making friends." What I slowly began to realize was that Zachary was not playing *with* the other children, but *beside* them. If they ran, he ran. If they screamed, he screamed; and so on. Zachary had mastered the skill of imitation but not of interaction.

Classroom activities were not going so well, either. Zachary's teacher began to complain that he was very inattentive. This was confusing to us. Zachary did not exhibit typical attention-deficit/hyperactivity disorder (ADHD) symptoms. He was not impulsive, nor was he distracted by external stimuli. He simply could not attend to activities that did not interest him.

One night, while I was reading with Zachary, he became extremely fidgety. I talked to him about paying attention in school. He looked up at me with shock in his eyes and said, "Mommy, I don't know what you're talking about. I thought I *was* paying attention in school." At that moment I knew something was very wrong. For the next two weeks, Zachary was petrified to go to school—not because he thought that he would get into trouble for not paying attention, but because he was worried that he wouldn't be paying attention and he wouldn't even know it.

First grade continued in an extremely haphazard manner. Zachary had the basic prereading skills to read, but he couldn't read. He had been able to add single digits since he was two, but now all of a sudden he wasn't able to grasp even the simplest math concepts. However, Zachary was motivated to make friends, and he made two friends whom he keeps in touch with even today.

The Breakthrough

During the fall of that school year, I took a trip to Boston to attend a conference. Many of the presenters were faculty members of Harvard Medical School. I was lucky enough to get a few moments with a psychiatrist, Dr. Martin Teicher, and tell him about Zachary's poor social skills, poor coping skills, inattentiveness, extremely intrusive obsessions, and exquisite ability to draw in three dimensions since the age of three.

Dr. Teicher suggested a possible diagnosis of Asperger's syndrome. I came home from my trip and immediately purchased Tony Attwood's book *Asperger's Syndrome: A Guide for Parents and Professionals*. It was both a relief and a heartache. I was sure that Dr. Attwood had used my son to write his book. Now I had a gut instinct, but I needed a diagnosis, and a diagnosis of Asperger's syndrome I did receive.

I won't ever forget that day. I felt as though someone had actually ripped out part of my heart and then told me it was my job to fill it back up again. I sat in a chair in the corner of the family room for four straight days, not talking, just thinking, in a severe state of grief. Then I realized that nothing was going to get done unless I stood up, got dressed, and began to take control. The ball began to roll as we set up the following:

- Assessments
- An individualized education plan (IEP) created by a school team that included academic goals, support services and assistance, and special accommodations
- Occupational therapy for sensory integration, fine motor skills, and attention to task
- Speech and language therapy to focus on social skills and conversational language
- Adaptive physical education to focus on gross motor skills
- An aide to assist with appropriate peer interaction, anxiety, and depression

- Talk therapy
- Psychopharmacology

I was the queen of early intervention, and as far as I could tell, I had six years to make up for. I had to hurry.

As first grade was coming to a close, the academics began to click. Zachary read beautifully, and although math continued to be a struggle, he was able to stay with his class as long as he had extra help. These advances were not a result of anything his father or I did. We had been providing academic intervention the entire time, but only when Zachary was good and ready was he able to access the skills that he had all along.

Social skills and coping skills were another matter. They required constant intervention, monitoring, and modeling. To this day they are the two developmental processes that determine Zachary's successes, disappointments, and sense of self-worth. They are a never-ending puzzle, and that is where this story really begins.

The following chapters describe the challenges that a child with Asperger's syndrome faces on a daily basis and the medication protocol for such children. Zachary's story and the stories of children in my professional life are woven throughout the book to provide you with concrete examples of clinical symptoms. The examples will also show strategies and interventions that have been successful and those that have not. Most of the strategies were based on Zachary's perceptions of the world. Those that were not will be very apparent to the reader, because they did not prove to be very effective.

In 2008, one of the "Top Ten Autism Research Events" listed by Autism Speaks was "Recovery from Autism Spectrum Disorder." Autism spectrum disorder was previously known as a disorder for which there was no cure. However, research has now placed the percentage of those who recover in the 3 percent to 25 percent range. Recovery is defined as having had clearly defined autistic spectrum disorder but currently no longer meeting the criteria. The research points out that the majority of children who are considered recovered had early intensive behavior intervention as well as characteristics that would predict outcomes such as higher IQ, receptive language ability, verbal and motor imitation, and motor development, and they were diagnosed at an early age. I see many children who have "recovered," but that doesn't necessarily mean that there aren't times they don't struggle with the remnants of the syndrome in social groups, novel situations, and changes in their routines. My definition of "recovered" is that you once had something, such as cancer, and now there are no longer any signs of the illness. Yes, my definition differs a bit from the one above, but if I choose the 2008 definition, then Zachary has recovered. He would no longer meet the criteria for Asperger's syndrome or autistic spectrum disorder.

2

Diagnostic Challenges in Asperger's Syndrome

Asperger's syndrome is a challenging diagnosis to make in the English-speaking world. Though similar to autism, and well-known in German-language literature, it began to appear in the diagnostic literature in the English-speaking world only in 1994. There are several instances of a child receiving a variety of incorrect diagnoses and therefore being treated incorrectly. In such cases the critical time for early intervention is lost. The delay in diagnosis can have a significant effect on the mental state and the academic progress of the individual with Asperger's syndrome.

Medical Perspective

Asperger's syndrome is a neuropsychiatric disorder characterized by a severe and sustained impairment in social interaction and communication and by a focus of interest on one area to the exclusion of others. In addition to these core symptoms, one of the challenging situations in Asperger's syndrome is the frequent occurrence of aggression, impulsivity, self-injury, poor frustration tolerance, inability to work in a structured environment, obsessive thoughts, and compulsive behavior.

Such behaviors bring parents to my (Syed's) office to seek psychopharmacological intervention and other help. There is clear evidence that ADHD, mood disorders (particularly depression), anxiety, and obsessive-compulsive disorder are sometimes difficult to distinguish from the core and innate symptoms of Asperger's syndrome. This can complicate the lives of Asperger's syndrome individuals and their parents, and it presents unique challenges to the clinician.

Sometimes one of these other psychiatric conditions appears in conjunction with Asperger's syndrome; at other times Asperger's syndrome individuals are misdiagnosed. Information that parents provide, such as a lack of social reciprocity or isolated hyper-focused interests, may be missed or ignored by the clinician. Instead, he or she might focus on mood, inattention, and anxiety, thereby giving a diagnosis based on one piece of the puzzle rather than the whole picture. Consistently poor social skills and little motivation for interactions with people of a similar age are often initially apparent and should be explored in depth. It has been my observation that children who are referred with Asperger's syndrome are usually older than children who are referred with other forms of autism.

It is important to take a detailed history from the parents or guardians. Collateral information may be collected from counselors, coaches, and teachers. It is absolutely essential to speak with all the adults involved in the social, emotional, and academic development of the child in order to make an appropriate diagnosis of Asperger's syndrome. Children with Asperger's syndrome often function much better in relationships with adults and with younger children than with their peers.

Direct observation of the child is, of course, important in making an appropriate diagnosis. However, the first time I meet the parents, I do not have them bring the child with them. Nothing will be accomplished if the child is not able to sit still while I speak with the parents. So I meet with the parents alone and have them bring a picture of the child. I evaluate the parents' presentation carefully. If the child were a high-functioning adolescent, then I might meet with him or her first. However, I don't believe that the issue of confidentiality is compromised if I meet with the parents alone first.

I ask the parents ahead of time to write me a letter, letting me know in their own words where the child is coming from, what he or she is doing, and where he or she seems to be going. I want them to focus on the child's strengths as well as weaknesses. This is the only item that I read before the first visit with the parents; I do not read any reports, evaluations, or questionnaires from other people at this time. The parents' description helps me to focus on the interview and build a picture of the child's predisposition and any precipitant factors.

In the second session, I spend time alone with the child. I prefer that the parents not be in the room, but sometimes their presence is necessary. I observe the physical features of the child's face and note any facial dysmorphology (malformation) by carefully examining the placement of the eyes, the ears, the lips, and the filtrum (the vertical groove in the median portion of the upper lip). Most of these facial dysmorphology features are more common in autism than in Asperger's syndrome. I identify whether the child has a large head or a small head. I note how the child walks, how (or if) the child establishes eye contact, and if the child has anticipatory anxiety. I use this time to talk with the child and to do some evaluation in a play setting.

By the third session I have read any reports and have spoken with the child's teachers, counselors, and other service providers. During this meeting the parents and I talk about short-term, midterm, and long-term goals. Most of the time the children are in crisis at this point, and the primary focus must be the stabilization of the child. Unfortunately, once the child is stabilized, a teacher will often think that now the child can make up for the missed schoolwork. This is a recipe for disaster. My formula for intervention is crisis intervention, stabilization, consolidation (so as not to lose the gains achieved in stabilization), and then growth and development.

Since a number of children with Asperger's syndrome have neurological issues, including the possibility of seizures, I might request a neurological consultation at this time. In addition, I might request an occupational therapy assessment or a language and speech assessment. This has to be done with a team approach. The team should consist of the parents, a child neurologist (if necessary), a child psychiatrist, a child psychologist, a social worker, a teacher, a language and speech pathologist, and any other related service providers. A developmental pediatrician should lead the team, but that is unfortunately not the current model. The child psychiatrist usually leads the team, at present. A developmental pediatrician would be an asset because of the issue of comorbidity (having other medical conditions in combination with Asperger's syndrome).

Each of my evaluations takes between three and four hours. I cannot see a child or the parents in forty-five minutes and prescribe medication. I need time to think and reflect. How much of the child's behavior is nature, and how much is nurture? How much is actually unhealthy rather than simply unusual or even eccentric? If I cannot decipher these issues, I cannot define the dichotomies. I look very clearly at the genetic history and at all the biological, psychological, spiritual, educational, and social components. My model consists of what I call the four Ps: predisposition, precipitant, perpetuation, and protective factors. I will explain each of in terms of the following case study.

I have a twenty-two-year-old patient who had straight A's in high school and went directly to college. Then he began to fall apart. His parents thought that everything was fine: he had good grades; he was just shy; he wanted his privacy. Unfortunately, this scenario occurs all too often. If a child is doing well in school but is private and quiet, he may just be an introvert, and that's fine. However, there were further indications that he was actually suffering from "behavior inhibition," which is part of an anxiety spectrum disorder. The symptoms of this are a slow heart rate and a tendency to shut down emotionally in novel situations.

The young man was diagnosed with Asperger's syndrome rather than autism, anxiety disorder, or depression. However, he had good mental intellectual capacities, which hid his innate deficits in social communication, affective reciprocity, and theory of mind (the ability to know another person's emotional and mental state, defined as empathy in real-life terms). A final diagnosis in adulthood is quite difficult, and many factors come into play.

Let us explore this case further by using the four Ps:

Predisposition
- Genetic predisposition: His grandmother and his mother both suffer from depression, and his mother is on Paxil.
- Psychological predisposition: He is very shy.
- Social predisposition: He is very isolated.

Precipitant (Why has this person come to me now, at twenty-two years of age?)
- Biological precipitant: He has a substance abuse problem.
- Psychological precipitant: He has no meaningful relationships.
- Social precipitant: He has no social interactions.

Perpetuation
- Biological perpetuation: Substance abuse is making the situation worse, and his depression is not being treated.
- Psychological perpetuation: No one is addressing his social anxiety.
- Social perpetuation: He spends all day in school and all evening in his room by himself.

Protective Factors

- Biological protective factors: He is intelligent. His mother has responded to medication for depression.
- Psychological protective factor: He agrees to try therapy and sees the potential benefit.
- Social protective factor: He has some understanding that he would benefit from social groups.

It was unfortunate that this young man had not received any early intervention. Had he received biological, psychological, social, educational, and spiritual intervention at an early age, he might be having a more successful outcome as a young adult. I continued to work with him and his family with the use of the medication Paxil. I chose this medication primarily to target his social anxiety and to improve his affective reciprocity, social communication, and theory of mind. He began to participate in a social skills group that focused on vocational training rather than a college education, and as a result he made a significant improvement in his career choices and feelings of self-worth. His obsessive-compulsive symptoms were channeled into an area of interest in his work as an apprentice repairer of antique clocks. He works full-time to this day.

Early intervention is ideal, but it is not always the reality; however, this doesn't mean that all hope is lost. Intervention at any time is beneficial, especially if it focuses on social skills, vocational training in the individual's area of strength, communication skills, and coping skills.

Medical Intervention

Families should first try nonmedical means of intervention, such as family therapy, behavior modification, and individual psychotherapy. There are no medications specifically for Asperger's syndrome. The FDA approved risperidone and Abilify for severe tantrums, severe irritability, and aggression in autism. A chemical restraint should be used only if there is approximately a 60 percent response rate and only when psychosocial interventions have not produced any results. If you have a child who has to wear a helmet because of self-injurious behavior, then physical restraint is not effective. If you have a child who bites his or her hands until the bone is visible, then a chemical restraint is necessary. These are examples from severe autism; in Asperger's it is more common to see significant challenging behaviors in the domain of irritability and aggression directed toward others or occasionally toward oneself.

In high-functioning children and adolescents with Asperger's syndrome, comorbid ADHD, obsessive-compulsive disorder (OCD), and depression are common. Appropriate psychotherapy has to be a part of the intervention. Just prescribing medication is not beneficial. Medication intervention should be decided on after the parents have exhausted the educational milieu with observation and with restructuring and enhancing the coping skills of the patient and the family.

Judicious use of medication and the implementation of therapy will allow a child to learn the necessary coping skills for attaining appropriate behavior and quality of life. In certain cases, these skills might not be accessible without the assistance of medication. The long-term risks of medication usage have not been determined, however. Prolonged use of medication increases the chances of serious side effects. Although these medications are usually safe, their long-term usage requires an evaluation of risk versus benefit.

Many parents think that once children are on medication, they must always be on medication, and this is not always true. It is a protocol of my practice that every child takes a "holiday" from medication during the summer after approximately one year of usage. I would prefer that the time off be during the school year, but most parents and teachers do not agree with this.

After the holiday from medication, approximately 15 to 20 percent of my patients do not need to start taking medication again. The other 80 to 85 percent do. This tells me that the holiday is a necessary part of the treatment protocol, and it shows the parents that the risk is balanced by objective benefits. It is important to remember that a child's brain, along with his or her anatomy and physiology in general, is still developing. A vigilant reevaluation of treatment goals and objectives during this growth and development is therefore critical.

Determining if and when medication is necessary requires objective and valid rating scales to be completed by the child's teacher. It is necessary to see all the data from a variety of observers in the child's life. Special focus is given to symptoms of irritability, temper tantrums, focus and attention, the ability to follow through in one's actions, behavioral disturbance, and aggression. Medication is often necessary in the school setting due to behavioral issues. For instance, a child cannot be allowed to bite another child, and if nonmedication interventions have not worked, then medication must be weighed as a viable option.

High-Functioning Autism versus Asperger's Syndrome

The terms *high-functioning autism* and *Asperger's syndrome* began to be used in the English-speaking world at approximately the same time. Lorna Wing came up with the term *Asperger's syndrome* when she translated the classic book on the subject by Hans Asperger from German to English in 1981. M. K. De Myer, J. N. Hingtgen, and R. K. Jackson came up with the term *high-functioning autism* in the same year.

This has led to a great deal of confusion. High-functioning autism has classically been described as a condition in which an individual shows signs of autism in early childhood but later develops greater social, communication, and adaptive behavior skills (sometimes in response to interventions). In contrast, Asperger's syndrome has classically been described as a condition in which an individual has social and communication difficulties and restricted interest but a high intellectual level. Sometimes the distinction is purely academic.

Does the label really make a difference in the clinical management of these individual? The answer is that perhaps it doesn't. A study done in 2004 examined the past and present behavior profiles of children with high-functioning autism and Asperger's syndrome and found them to be indistinguishable in their overall presentation and clinical challenges.

Although the diagnosis of Asperger's syndrome is often given to individuals with average IQs, other individuals with the diagnosis have high IQs or score as mildly retarded. It is not uncommon for children with Asperger's syndrome to have highly developed rote skills, such as decoding and computation, but to have difficulty with application, such as reading comprehension and word problems. Clinical practice in the United States leans more toward a diagnosis of high-functioning autism rather than Asperger's syndrome, because people with high-functioning autism tend to get more services, such as behavior intervention, speech and language therapy, and occupational therapy.

Our special-education communities continue to be behind the times in recognizing the significant impairment of a child with Asperger's syndrome. This is usually because the child has average or above-average cognitive ability and at times does very well in school. What the special-education agencies and school personnel fail to realize is that social impairment, severe anxiety, and depression have a major impact on a child's developmental ability, regardless of academic ability. Until Asperger's syndrome is recognized as a significant and unique disability in the spectrum of autistic disorders, one must often struggle just to receive the services that the child rightfully deserves and needs. If that means accepting a diagnosis on paper of autism rather than Asperger's syndrome, so be it.

The Challenges of Diagnosing Asperger's Syndrome in Girls

Girls present an extremely challenging profile in the diagnosis of Asperger's syndrome. They can easily be overlooked as simply having a difficult time in relationships and communication because of the social milieu.

Girls' camouflaging strategies in peer interactions occasionally make their social errors inconspicuous. Their literal thinking, their inability to see another's perspective in a situation, and their affective reciprocity are more subtle. They sometimes require a long diagnostic workup and are often diagnosed at a much later age than their male counterparts, because their symptoms can remain hidden for decades. Girls with Asperger's syndrome often have the ability to blend into larger groups in order to function on the periphery of social interactions. Many of them describe themselves as somebody who is sitting on the outside looking in.

Girls with Asperger's syndrome often do not manifest conduct disorder issues, such as verbal defiance, tantrums, and obstinacy, which are common in adolescent males. Because the girls have no apparent conduct disorder or outward behavioral difficulties and they are polite and mannerly, they are less noticeable to their teachers. They may also have a spirit of peer cooperation and social inclusion at school. Thus, the overall social milieu in the day-to-day life among girls may make the diagnostic workup difficult.

Although the language and cognitive profile of girls can be similar to that of boys, their special interests might not be as overly visible as abnormal or unusual. A boy with Asperger's syndrome might be labeled as a little professor who has an advanced vocabulary and knowledge about isolated odd subjects, whereas a girl might be described as a little philosopher who occasionally has a great deal of cognitive ability to think in depth about social situations, thereby appearing as simply analytical and wise beyond her years rather than as having a social challenge. Girls with Asperger's syndrome spend a significant amount of time concretely analyzing social interactions rather than simply responding to the feeling of them, as their typical peers do.

Furthermore, the motor and coordination problems that we often see in boys with Asperger's syndrome might not be that evident in girls because of less emphasis on sports in the lives of many girls. Therefore, adults do not tend to notice the girls' challenges at an early age, which means that a diagnosis is not made until later and an extremely important window for early intervention is closed.

ADHD Symptomatology Confusion

Children often have impulsive behaviors that coexist in Asperger's syndrome and ADHD. It is important to note that the same individual can have both conditions. However, many professionals who are more familiar with the symptoms of ADHD often diagnose a child with ADHD when a comorbid diagnosis would be more appropriate.

In my (Syed's) experience, more than 50 percent of misdiagnoses of Asperger's syndrome were made in ADHD clinics. There is often a conflict between the parents' and the teacher's report on the degree and quality of the inattentive behavior.

However, in Asperger's syndrome, one notices a limited interest, a greater degree of fixation on or obsession with certain topics, and resistance in transitioning to other activities. There is usually an inability to focus attention on books or other media because they are gathering information about circumscribed or very detailed interests to the point of exclusion of all other activities. Reading tends out to be more rote than comprehending.

One has to be cautious about a comorbid ADHD-Asperger's diagnosis. Individuals with Asperger's syndrome are often called spacey when they are not focusing on things that interest them, and this is not typical of ADHD. However, when asked to respond to a topic-related question, the child is usually able to respond correctly even though he or she appeared inattentive. Eye contact tends to be poor, affect is flat, and these children are often described as being in a world of their own. These are some of the cognitive symptoms of Asperger's syndrome, not ADHD.

A lack of motivation and connectedness are specific to Asperger's syndrome. Children with ADHD often exhibit social problems, but they are considered secondary to the core symptoms of ADHD: hyperactivity, impulsivity, and/or inattention in two or more settings that cause a disturbance—vocationally, socially, educationally, and/or academically. The social problems of ADHD also appear later in development and do not usually have the odd quality that they do in Asperger's syndrome.

Preoccupations, Perseverations, and Fixations

Preoccupations, perseverations, fixations, and other OCD-like behaviors are sometimes very difficult to delineate. Where is the boundary between an atypical but healthy childhood interest and the intense circumscribed or limited interest found in Asperger's syndrome? When does a preoccupation with the latest toy or computer game become excessive? The timing, the intensity, and the nature of the circumscribing interest provide unique clues for detecting Asperger's syndrome. A child who has read the latest Harry Potter book twenty times in two weeks is not reading for meaning. This intensity is beyond simple obsessive-compulsiveness and has the quality that is frequently found in Asperger's syndrome.

Nuances in obsessions are noted in Asperger's syndrome. Memorization of map details, districts, area codes, or bus stops are examples of the sorts of odd interests seen in Asperger's syndrome. These interests are apparent in conversations with

Asperger's individuals, who can and will overwhelm the listener with detailed information and will even attempt to force this interest on others. The normal give-and-take in social situations is seldom seen. This frequently leads to the alienation of individuals who do not share the interests. The "lecturing" children then gravitate toward younger children, who are more receptive to and tolerant of the plethora of data, which can be meaningless to them. Parents can find it increasingly difficult to develop the right kind of social milieu for their children with Asperger's syndrome.

People with Asperger's syndrome often avoid team sports, because these require a high degree of social interaction, motivation, commitment, and physical coordination. Even those rare individuals with Asperger's who are interested in sports have little or no inclination to participate in them; they would rather just memorize the statistics associated with the sport.

These types of intense unusual preoccupations are often the first symptoms that catch the attention of the parents. For instance, an eighteen-month-old child may be preoccupied by the ringing of a phone or the sound of a vacuum cleaner or a three-year-old might pick up bottle tops and collect them, to the exclusion of any other activity.

Asperger's syndrome can be comorbid with OCD and include checking, counting, and similar preoccupations, but these are mostly syntonic (in emotional equilibrium and responsive to the environment). The repetitive behavior of some of these activities usually shows up in children with classic Asperger's syndrome but can also be seen in its variants or less intense forms. Lining up one's toys repeatedly and spinning the wheels of a toy vehicle repeatedly instead of playing with them in an interactive or reciprocal way are a few examples of odd play or play outside of the domain of normal play. Focusing for long periods on the glow of the flame and looking for hours at flickering lights to the exclusion of the daily routines of life are a few examples of OCD type of behavior. Constant opening and closing of doors or substimulatory behaviors such as head-flapping, head-banging, and head-rocking can also be seen. Echolalia is also occasionally observed in many Asperger's syndrome individuals. Some of these activities do disappear as the child grows older, but some remain and are even replaced by other substimulatory behavior.

Anxiety Spectrum Disorder

Many children with Asperger's syndrome receive a diagnosis of generalized anxiety and panic attacks. The key to the diagnosis of Asperger's syndrome is the manifestation of anxiety in specific social situations, such as a birthday party or a playdate that overwhelms or bewilders these children. This anxiety is not related to internal conflict, so it can be alleviated by developing social skills and by learning how to manipulate the environment to make it less threatening, such as through the use of prediction, social scripts, and role-playing.

An individual with Asperger's syndrome might want to connect with others but not know how. This can lead to a situation in which he or she reacts with a fight, flight, fright, or freeze. Anxiety occasionally manifests in an effort to be a class clown. An individual with Asperger's syndrome might find this to be the only way of having any kind of peer acceptance.

Home-to-School Perspective

Many, if not most, of the students whom I work with have multiple diagnoses. The most common comorbid diagnoses along with Asperger's syndrome seem to be anxiety disorder, depression, obsessive compulsive disorder and ADD, or ADHD and behavioral disorders. Unfortunately, most of these additional diagnoses present in the child's behavior. ADHD can cause behavior that looks like inattentiveness: constant movement, poor social skills, and impulsive reactions or actions. Anxiety disorder can also cause impulsive behavior, noncompliance at home and at school, meltdowns that result in tantruming, a short fuse, excessive questioning, and an increase in obsessive-compulsive behaviors. Depression can present as noncompliance, a lack of motivation that can be seen as laziness, inattentiveness, poor social skills, an unwillingness to interact with others, a short fuse, and debilitating sadness. Obsessive-compulsive disorder involves difficulties with transitions, repetitive thoughts, and behaviors that significantly impact the child's ability to engage in daily activity: poor social skills, impaired conversational skills, excessive questioning, and heightened anxiety. Behavior disorders can be diagnosed simultaneously; however, many of the above diagnoses result in maladaptive behavior as a symptom of the pathology.

As you can see, many if not all of these diagnostic symptoms overlap with the single diagnosis of Asperger's syndrome. Therefore, it can be extremely difficult to determine if the behavioral presentation is a secondary diagnosis or simply a symptom of the primary diagnosis. It is of utmost importance that those working directly with the child provide interventions (please see separate chapters) that address the underlying cause of the behavior, and not simply respond to just the symptom.

3

Comorbid Disorders: Isn't Having Just Asperger's Syndrome Enough?

As many as one in four individuals with Asperger's syndrome has some other medical condition as well; this is called *comorbidity*. Recent studies of Asperger's syndrome show that in children with normal to high IQs, as many as one in six has an associated medical disorder. This indicates an essential need for care with a specialist who has expertise in these special-needs children, such as a developmental pediatrician or a physician with experience in treating comorbidity with Asperger's syndrome.

General Medical Perspective

In one group of studies, 70 percent of the children with Asperger's syndrome also had anxiety or depression; 60 to 70 percent had

ADHD, 75 to 80 percent had obsessive-compulsive disorder, 11 to 15 percent had a tic-related disorder, and 35 to 40 percent had a behavior disorder related to Asperger's syndrome but not the core part of the disorder itself.

There is an overrepresentation of psychiatric disorders in children who have been diagnosed with Asperger's syndrome. Schizophrenia is a rare possibility; children with Asperger's syndrome are more vulnerable to schizophrenia and psychosis in general. Parents should always ask the doctor, "What else could my child have? Does Asperger's syndrome explain my child's complete lack of attention in the classroom, or does he or she have something else?"

When children are diagnosed with both Asperger's syndrome and either ADHD or a tic disorder, the question is how much of the maladaptive behavior can actually be controlled by the child and whether it is actually due to the impulsivity of ADHD or the tic-related disorder.

Each issue of comorbidity is examined below.

Epilepsy

Epilepsy occurs in childhood autism at the rate of 20 to 25 percent. The exact incidence in Asperger's disorder is not known. As we do take Asperger's as a part of larger autistic spectrum disorders, it is important to be aware of the possibility of seizures and their various presentations in this syndrome. The most common variants are absence, or petit mal, seizures, rather than classic tonic-clonic, or grand mal, seizures. Absence seizures include episodic periods of prolonged staring, inattentiveness, and confusion.

Seizures are usually found to occur in adolescents (eleven to nineteen years old) with autistic spectrum disorder as benign absence seizures. Although epilepsy or seizure disorder is common in all forms of autism, it appears to be rarer in Asperger's syndrome— but it still occurs at a higher rate than in the general public.

It is hypothesized that individuals with Asperger's syndrome who have an abnormally large head (macrocephaly) tend to have a higher incidence of epilepsy.

The treatment of epilepsy in Asperger's syndrome can be challenging. Most of the drugs used in Asperger's syndrome—especially risperidone, the recently FDA-approved antipsychotic drug for irritability, aggression, and other issues in autism—can increase the chances of seizure in many vulnerable individuals.

The classic drug for the treatment of seizures is Depakote (divalproex sodium) or Depakene (valproic acid). It not only alleviates or ameliorates seizures but in many situations also reduces poor impulse control, aggression, self-injurious behavior, and irritability.

Tegretol (carbamazepine) is another drug that is frequently used to control seizures in individuals with Asperger's syndrome. It is important that the psychiatrist or the pediatrician work collaboratively with a child neurologist in the treatment of these children. Some patients require specialized tests of the brain, such as the electroencephalogram (EEG). The level of medication in the blood must also be monitored through frequent blood tests.

Hearing Deficits

Moderate hearing deficits occur in a small minority of children with Asperger's syndrome, and complete deafness is present in fewer individuals (though still more than in the general population). Both have important clinical implications. In contrast, acoustic hypersensitivity, or extreme sensitivity to noise or voices, is common, occurring in about 30 percent of children with Asperger's syndrome. It is hypothesized that many of these sound-sensitive children have the ability to hear voices from distances that are beyond normal human capability.

Hearing tests should be done on a regular basis because of the importance of communication, speech, and language issues in Asperger's syndrome. A child with a partial hearing deficit or complete deafness is at a disadvantage in acquiring speech and language skills and will require early intervention programs. If a hearing test elicits normal hearing in a child who appears deaf, Asperger's syndrome should be suspected; ADHD or a specific speech and language disorder, such as Landau-Kleffner syndrome, might also be the correct diagnosis.

Many children with hearing deficits have been wrongfully diagnosed as autistic when the only problem was the lack of detection of sound. In addition, many fully hearing individuals who are not communicating are wrongly considered to be deaf when their main issue is actually Asperger's syndrome.

Visual Deficits

Visual deficits are common in Asperger's syndrome, but the exact statistics are unknown. There are certain types of congenital blindness with brain damage, such as retinopathy of prematurity (abnormal blood vessel development in the retinas of premature infants), which are strongly associated with Asperger's syndrome. Nearsightedness and farsightedness are also associated; they should be evaluated early and treated appropriately and aggressively.

Genetic Disorders

The three most common brain disorders in children with an IQ of 50 are called tuberous sclerosis, fragile X syndrome, and partial tetrasomy 15. These are found in 15 to 20 percent of all children with core autism. Fragile X syndrome, a genetic condition involving changes in part of the X chromosome, is an issue with a few of the girls who meet the diagnostic criteria of Asperger's syndrome. All boys with fragile X syndrome tend to be mentally retarded, but girls with full-blown fragile X syndrome may be of normal IQ.

Other common genetic conditions in autism that affect intellectual functioning are Moebius syndrome, 22q11 deletion syndrome, Angelman syndrome, and sex chromosome abnormalities. In the past, rubella embryopathy and phenylketonuria (PKU) have been significant.

Some of these conditions have been resolved in the industrialized parts of the world with early birth screening, such as in the case of phenylketonuria. These genetic disorders, though relatively uncommon in Asperger's, should be screened in the assessment for Asperger's syndrome, because they require specialized medical care. Genetic disorders are much more common in other forms of autism than in Asperger's syndrome.

Intellectual Disabilities and Learning Disorders

Mental retardation occurs in 60 to 70 percent of children with autism, but it is, by definition, not present in the form of autism that is Asperger's syndrome. Dyscalculia (a math learning disability), dyslexia (a reading disability in which letters are transposed), and nonverbal learning disabilities are associated with Asperger's syndrome.

Tic Disorder versus ADHD

Tic disorder or ADHD with Asperger's syndrome is a difficult comorbidity to treat. Tics are movements that mimic normal behavior in a sustained manner. Differentiating tics from ADHD is not a problem in itself; the problem arises when impulsivity is involved. Medication for tics can make the ADHD symptomatology worse, and the treatment for ADHD can make tics increase. Tic disorder medications block the dopamine receptors, whereas the medications that enhance the dopamine receptors are used to treat ADHD.

In addition, many tic-like behaviors can mimic undiagnosed seizures. Some patients have been diagnosed with tic disorder only to find out that they are having small partial seizures. Only an EEG can accurately determine this diagnosis, but unless the patient is having brain activity during the EEG, the EEG will not identify the partial seizure. Therefore, seventy-two-hour EEG evaluation (electrical mapping of the brain) is needed.

Confusing Schizophrenia and Asperger's Syndrome

Personality disorders have sometimes have been defined as issues in autistic adolescents. Many children with Asperger's syndrome have been misdiagnosed with schizophreniform (a time-limited schizophrenia) or schizoid personality disorder.

Hans Asperger spent a great deal of time differentiating Asperger's syndrome from schizophrenia. Nevertheless, in clinical practice, one is often challenged to find schizophrenia over and above an established Asperger's syndrome. The problem manifests as confusion with signs of paranoia. It appears to be a misinterpretation of real experiences of the self and of responses to real social experiences in children with Asperger's syndrome.

Early teasing and deliberate provocative bullying can sometimes cause an individual with Asperger's syndrome to develop suspicion of others, thereby perceiving the teasing as malicious intent by all people, by people in a position of authority, or by large groups of people. This has to be corrected by explanation and by trying to restructure the social milieu in which the situations occur.

Although there are no data to support an overrepresentation of schizophrenia, many adolescents with Asperger's do say that they hear an inner voice telling them what to do. This is a concrete representation of the human unconscious and is not necessarily a depiction of paranoia or hallucination. The attribution of psychotic delusion must be clearly differentiated in people with Asperger's syndrome. In order to cope with the real world and be able to lead their lives, people with Asperger's syndrome tend to create a fantasy life with imaginary friends and imaginary worlds in which they are properly understood. The contrast between the real world and the imaginary world can become quite acute and bizarre in adolescents and can sometime lead to confusion with schizophrenia.

Individuals with Asperger's syndrome tend to switch topics, causing a misinterpretation on the part of the evaluator and leading to a diagnosis of psychosis. Some individuals do have a psychotic conversion and develop schizophrenia with Asperger's syndrome, but the number of such individuals remains very small.

Medical Intervention

Depakene (valproic acid), Depakote (divalproex sodium), and Tegretol (carbamazepine) are classic antiseizure medications that have frequently been used in treating the symptoms of aggression in Asperger's syndrome. They have been found to be beneficial in children with Asperger's syndrome and a comorbid diagnosis of seizure disorder. There are no double-blind controlled studies for their efficacy, however, and their use is limited to open-label studies with experts who have experience in the use of these drugs. The open-label trials of valproic acid and divalproex sodium have shown them to improve aggression and repetitive behavior.

There are safety issues related to the use of these drugs, and frequent monitoring is essential in the form of liver function tests, blood tests, and bone marrow function tests.

A double-blind placebo-controlled trial with Lamictal (lamotrigine), another antiseizure drug, has not shown it to be efficacious in controlling the aggressive behaviors in Asperger's syndrome. It has, however, been shown to be useful in children with Asperger's with labile mood or at times treatment-resistant depression.

Hyperactivity and impulsivity are generally treated with non-stimulant medications like Strattera and Intuniv (the long-acting form of a recently approved FDA medication for the treatment of the core symptoms of ADHD). Mood lability, aggressiveness, and self-injurious behavior are treated with Depakene (valproic acid), Tegretol (carbamazapine), and antipsychotics such as Risperdal and Zyprexa (olanzapine). Anxiety, panic, depression, and OCD symptoms respond well to selective serotonin reuptake inhibitors (SSRIs), or antidepressants, and Buspar (buspirone), an antianxiety drug.

Another study surveyed fifty families on their use of minocycline, an old antibiotic, in fragile X syndrome, which one sees sometimes in pure autism. About 70 percent had experienced improvements in anxiety and behavioral symptoms with very few side effects (mainly gastrointestinal problems and a graying of the teeth).

These findings are relevant only to girls with fragile X syndrome, however, because (as mentioned earlier) only girls can have fragile X syndrome comorbid with Asperger's syndrome, as they may have a normal IQ.

4

The Parents' Guide to Recognizing and Diagnosing Asperger's Syndrome

Hans Asperger, a Viennese pediatrician, struggled with identifying, describing, and labeling boys with unique and intriguing characteristics. In 1943, he studied a small group of boys with the following characteristics: qualitative impairment in social interactions, a lack of spontaneous speech and an inability to maintain the topics of a given conversation, no social and emotional reciprocity, and a failure to develop peer relationships. He called this *autistic psychopathy*, which we would describe as a personality disorder.

At approximately the same time in the United States, Leo Kanner was taking note of similar characteristics with his own group of unique and interesting children. He found an impairment in the interpretation of social cues, no peer relationships, no spontaneous speech, no language development before the age of three, an inability to sustain conversations (if the children were verbal at all), and the use of stereotypical language. These children lacked an ability to engage in make-believe play, and most had significant cognitive impairment.

It was not until 1981 that Lorna Wing, a pediatric psychiatrist, wrote a paper combining the two sets of characteristics. While doing so, she realized that although many children exhibited classic autistic symptoms at an early age, as identified in Kanner's work, these children continued to develop fluent speech and a desire to socialize. After many hours with intensive early intervention, these children, who were originally socially aloof from their peers and were motivated only toward solitude, now wanted friends. In addition, their interests turned into significant repetitive thoughts about particular details, such as the drapes in a restaurant or how many pages there were in a day planner.

What does this all mean? Would Zachary have been one of Asperger's kids, one of Kanner's, or something in between, as Wing described? Does it matter? Does treatment depend on an accurate diagnosis, or does simply diagnosing a child with Asperger's syndrome suffice? I (Melinda) don't know the answer to this question. Is the syndrome a spectrum of behaviors, or do these behaviors form completely different diagnoses?

My thoughts, both personally and professionally, are that many of the characteristics do overlap; however, they manifest differently in each child, just as no two Fuji apples taste exactly the same. The closest you could get would be to buy two Fuji apples at the same time of the year from the same farmer whose crop received the same amount of sun, water, and nutrients. Even then the two apples would be different—but they are still both Fuji apples.

As difficult as it is to pinpoint the correct diagnosis on the autism spectrum, it is not difficult to identify the characteristics that will guide the clinician in that direction. Thus, armed with a few good questions for parents, teachers, and support personnel, you will at least have a starting point. It might not be a perfect diagnosis, but it will be something to create a plan by and work from, and sometimes that's as much as we can hope for.

I receive many phone calls from parents whose children have not yet been diagnosed with anything. They are not calling me for an assessment or a diagnosis, but only because I am a mom who has already had the experience and a professional who sees a variety of "Fuji apples." I listen to the parents' stories and wait to hear a varied but clear-cut list of characteristics. If I don't hear answers to the following pertinent questions, I begin to ask them myself:

- Does your child have friends?
- Does your child ask follow-up questions and stay on the same topic of conversation?
- Does your child initiate play with other children in an unstructured environment such as the park?
- Will your child respond with joy and acceptance to another child's initiation of play and conversation?
- Does your child have a specific talent that seems unusually advanced for his or her age?
- What happens if you pick your child up from school and decide to go to the market, but you haven't told him or her ahead of time? Will the child be okay with the change in plans?
- Is your child sensitive to noise, touch, and smells, such as scratchy clothes, chirping crickets, or the screech of car tires on the road?
- Is your child able to understand the physical and emotional pain of others, and does he or she respond appropriately to those feelings?
- Is your child aware when others are happy, upset, or angry? If so, what does he or she do during those times?
- Does your child take things literally, and is he or she able to understand implied meanings?

If the answer to most of these questions is no, or the child shows an inability to cope or respond appropriately within the abovementioned social situations, then I have a pretty good idea that I'm on the right track in making appropriate educational and medical recommendations. However, this last question is the deal breaker:

- Does your child have intense, unusual interests that he or she consistently and constantly talks about? For example, if the child's obsession is the vacuum cleaner or a roll of adhesive tape, does he or she talk about that item even when it is not in sight? Does he or she continue talking about the item regardless of others' obvious uninterest or boredom?

If the parents are bewildered, cannot relate to what I am asking, and don't understand the question, then that is a sign that we are on the wrong track. However, if the parent responds with "Yes, he's completely obsessed with cell division and won't talk about anything else," then I know we are on our way to a possible diagnosis of Asperger's syndrome. There is a fine line between being eccentric and growing up to be a scientific genius and presenting repetitive thoughts and behaviors that go beyond what would be considered normal. Many people do not like the term "normal," but I love it, since it gives a frame of reference. It is not uncommon for children to hyperfocus on one activity such as baseball or video games. The main difference between children who are neurotypical and those who have a disorder is that neurotypical children can be redirected to other activities without a great deal of anxiety or behavior. Neurotypical children do not necessarily talk about their interest during completely unrelated activities. Children with Asperger's syndrome struggle with all of the above. The transition from their current interest to another activity is extremely difficult and requires significant intervention beyond what would be required for a typical child. These children also struggle with understanding that no one is interested in cell division at a birthday party and with their inability to read the social cues of others, such as eye-rolling, turning away, or ending a conversation, as signs of disinterest. Mainstream obsessions are obviously much easier to disguise, but that doesn't mean that they aren't equally intrusive.

This assessment is not the be-all and end-all in diagnosing a child with Asperger's syndrome, but it is a quick and easy way for parents to determine if their child could have this condition. This quick survey does not take the place of a professional assessment and diagnosis by a clinician who specializes in this field; that information is invaluable. I tell parents all the time that a correct diagnosis will give them a different perspective from what they otherwise would have had, and it will assist them in making future decisions for their children.

Any child whose challenges are affecting his or her ability to develop socially, academically, and psychologically and be a contributing member of a social group needs intervention, regardless of a diagnosis. Genetic testing is a must in order to rule out any underlying genetic disorders that may be the cause of autistic symptomatology.

5

The Next Steps

Once you have a diagnosis, what do you do next? Unfortunately, when I (Melinda) received Zachary's diagnosis, no sooner was I given a detailed explanation of what was wrong with my child than the hour was up. I left the psychologist's office filled with questions, depression, and apprehension. I had to make an additional appointment just to ask all my questions. You might not know what questions to ask, or that you even *have* any questions, until you get home. That's okay. Read, research, ask questions, and make a list. Make another appointment with your psychologist or other practitioner to ask all your questions. In the interim, here are the first steps to follow:

1. Early intervention for toddlers has been shown to be effective for improving cognition, language, and adaptive behavior (Top 10 Autism Research Achievements of 2009, Autism Speaks—National Advocacy Agency). One of the most common early intervention programs is the Early

Start Denver Model, which combines Applied Behavior Analysis (ABA) teaching with play therapy in order to form a relationship with the child.

2. If your child is of school age, contact the local school your child attends. Inform the administrators of the diagnosis and request an individualized education plan (IEP) and assessments in the following areas: psychology, academics, speech and language, occupational therapy, and adaptive physical education. The IEP and the assessments have to be done within sixty days of your signing the assessment plan, so don't wait to sign. Please understand that just because you come in with outside assessments does not mean that your child will receive services. Every district has to complete its own assessment to determine eligibility for services, although it will take the outside assessments into consideration. In addition, simply having a diagnosis does not ensure eligibility for special education. Districts want to know if the child's disability impacts his or her ability to access the curriculum. For example, if the child is doing fine in school but is having trouble just at home, it will be extremely hard to receive services, because the disability is not impacting the child's access to the school-based education. As the parent, you need to advocate for the connection between home and school and help your team to understand that the environments overlap and one is not exclusive of the other.

3. Request all written reports before the IEP is finalized so that you can see the outcome and prepare any necessary argument. Remember, your argument always has to support the fact that your child's disability is impacting him or her in school.

4. If possible, have the professional who diagnosed your child attend the IEP session, preferably in person, but by phone or videoconference otherwise. You need support,

whether from the practitioner, an advocate, your spouse, or a friend.

5. Really think about what your child needs. More services are not always better. If the team is suggesting a service in the classroom, listen. It might be a more effective way to provide the service.

6. Contact your regional center or state agencies that provide services for children and adults with developmental disabilities. Please remember that these agencies are payers of last resort; they will assist you in obtaining services from your school district or your medical insurance before funding anything themselves. In addition, due to the downturn in the economy, social service agencies are cutting back what few services they did provide. Don't wait for your case manager to lay the services on the table so you can choose; this won't happen. You have to take the initiative and request what you want, such as respite services (a type of relief for parents), home behavior intervention, and so on. This process usually takes about six months, so start immediately and keep calling.

The Individuals with Disabilities Education Act (IDEA) authorizes federal funding for special-education and related services in states that accept these funds. There are certain conditions under which special-education and related services are to be provided. These are as follows:

- States and school districts offer a free and appropriate education (FAPE) to all children with disabilities between ages three and twenty-one. States and school districts identify, locate, and evaluate all children with disabilities, regardless of the severity of the disability, to determine which children are eligible for special-education and related services.

- Each child who receives services has an IEP that identifies the specific special-education and related services that must be provided to meet the child's needs. Members of the IEP team include, but are not limited to, the school administrator, the regular education teacher, the parents, the special education teacher, and all pertinent service providers whom the parent chooses to bring in addition to any outside professionals who have completed an assessment.

- To the maximum extent that is appropriate, children with disabilities must be educated with children who are not disabled. States and school districts must provide procedural safeguards to children with disabilities and their parents, including the right to a due process hearing, the right to appeal to a federal district court, and, at times, the right to attorney's fees.

IDEA requires the state to provide sufficient services for the child to benefit educationally from instruction and move successfully from grade to grade. IDEA does not require the state to provide services to *maximize* the potential of a child with a disability.

Placement Options

States and school districts are obligated to provide a scaffolding of educational placements and services for children depending on their needs, placing the child in the least restrictive environment that meets his or her specific needs. Therefore, education placements move from least restrictive to most restrictive, as follows:

- **General education with special-education support.** The student is placed in a general-education classroom on a typical campus with a credentialed special-education teacher to provide support. This support can be implemented in a variety of ways, depending on the student's needs, the school programming, and the district policy. The special educator can provide consultation to the regular-education teacher in terms of teaching methods, alternative assessments, and educational accommodations and modifications. The special educator can also provide direct service—that is, work directly with the student for a portion of the day, either in the regular-education class or in small-group or one-to-one instruction. This is sometimes called a resource teacher or a resource program. The child returns to spend the majority of the day in the typical classroom with children who are not receiving special-education services. General-education classes are usually quite large, ranging from twenty to thirty-five students, depending on the grade. The advantage of the general-education environment for the special-needs child is the exposure to typical activities and academic and social development among typical developing peers. The disadvantages are teachers who are not experienced in working with special-needs children, the intolerance of other students and teachers, and the feelings of the special-needs child that he or she is the only one who needs extra help or doesn't fit in. Full inclusion with support is successful if it is a team effort, with parents, administrators, regular-education and special-education teachers, and service providers all in agreement with the educational program and its consistent implementation. The classroom environment should be taken into consideration: typical peers and typical activities versus possibly less structure; a teacher who is familiar versus unfamiliar with the particular disability; and overstimulation caused by the classroom environment such as number of children, larger classroom space, and larger group instruction versus one-to-one or small-group instruction.

- **Special day class.** The special day class is a self-contained class on a general-education campus that serves students with special needs. All instruction is provided by a special-education teacher for the majority of the day. Although the students with disabilities are among themselves for the majority of the day, the general-education campus provides the opportunity for typical social activities, such as recess, lunch, assemblies, and extracurricular activities. There is also the possibility of mainstreaming into a regular-education class for a particular subject. The disadvantage is that many of these programs serve children of very different needs and a variety of different grades, so a special day class might not be geared specifically toward your child's needs, disability, or grade level.

- **Nonpublic school.** A nonpublic school is a school entirely for children with special needs. Most students are funded through the school district, which therefore makes it free of charge for the parents. A nonpublic school is considered a therapeutic environment, so all related services—such as counseling, adaptive physical education, speech and language therapy, and occupational therapy—are normally provided on the school site during school hours. This setting is especially beneficial when service providers are part of the IEP on a daily basis. Team meetings are much more conducive to this environment, simply because of logistics, which creates the opportunity for a more consistent program. In addition, the providers can assist on a moment's notice during particular situations or crises in order to remedy the issue and capture a teachable moment immediately. The students are taught by special educators in all state-required subjects throughout the day. The teachers generally have experience with the specific population with which they are working; however, that is not always the case. Special educators are in short supply across the country. The classes are smaller, with a much higher adult-to-student ratio, than in a special day class or a general-education setting. The disadvantage is that this placement is basically a special day program without any typical peers. It will then be your responsibility, as a parent, to make sure that your child has interactions with typical peers. Although social skills programs can and should be very specialized in this environment, one must take into consideration that typical responses to prompted interaction cannot be counted on; this makes it difficult, at times, to model and role-play interactions with others. When prompting a child with Asperger's syndrome to initiate a conversation with a group of typical children, one can be fairly certain that the typical response to "Can I play?" will be "We have too many kids already," "Wait until the next game," or "Yes, you can play." Knowing the possible answers ahead of time allows the teacher to prompt the child with appropriate responses. However, if the teacher is prompting a child to initiate play with a group of children who have the same challenges, the responses could vary a great deal, which makes it more difficult to role-play appropriate responses. Nonpublic schools offer a vast array of services and specialized instruction for their students.

- **Residential placement.** Residential placement is considered when parents have exhausted all other possibilities and the child is engaged in such significant behavioral issues that he or she is unable to develop socially and emotionally as part of a family and community or educationally as an integral member of the school environment in any of the above placements. At times, the need for intervention and consistent therapy is significant enough to warrant twenty-four-hour care in a therapeutic environment. This placement encompasses all education, social, emotional, and medical needs while the student is living at the residence.

An entire spectrum of placements is available to children with Asperger's syndrome. Every person who cares for and provides services to such a child needs to discuss the best options for the student at a particular time. No placement is perfect. One has to determine the symptoms and/or challenges that are of the utmost importance and base the decision solely on them.

Hospitalization

Currently, the criterion for hospitalization is danger to oneself, danger to others, grave disability, or needs not being met. At the moment, hospitalization is used only for severe tantrums, severe disturbance in behavior, or danger to oneself or others. Some people hope that in the future it will be possible for families and physicians to hospitalize children who are on a complicated cocktail of medications and who need to be weaned from them in a controlled setting to start over again. There are many children with Asperger's syndrome, in this view, who would require hospitalization to address complicated medication cocktails.

Inpatient psychiatric hospitalization has become acute-care intervention. No longer are we admitting children to psychiatric hospitals for a long period of time. Children might be admitted to an inpatient unit for significant depression, anxiety, and/or self-injurious behaviors. As soon as they are deemed stable, they are sent home; many times they have not been given enough time to exhibit the original behaviors that got them involuntarily admitted in the first place, such as self-injurious behaviors or aggression toward others. Nor have they had time to change medications effectively. Unfortunately, because of changes in the health care system, such as the lack of beds for psychiatric patients, resulting in waiting lists for those beds and insurance denials for longer stays, some parents are resorting to residential placement when hospitalization should, in my opinion, be the option instead.

When is the right time to hospitalize? When my son was finally hospitalized, it was after a year of reassuring myself that things would change, trying one strategy after another, and consulting additional specialists. Zachary's behavior became so intrusive, which included self-injurious behavior and severe anxiety and depression, that it did not allow us to function as a family, nor did it allow him to function as a child or as part of a bigger world. It is a frightening proposition to admit your child to a psychiatric hospital. You do not ever think that you are going to get to that point. However, there are times when it should be considered. When children become a danger to themselves or others, when they are not able to access their education, or when they are not able to maintain enough control to be a successful, contributing member of your family, maintain reasonable expectations for the age of the child. In other words, if your child is unable to participate in family meals, family activities, or school requirements on a daily basis because they are engaging in significant behaviors, then it is time to think about hospitalization.

In addition, difficult medication changes become quicker and easier during an inpatient stay rather than on an outpatient basis, when physicians must be called and parents must wait.

However, that being said, hospitalization can be quite traumatic for children. They are taken away from what is familiar to them. New rules are implemented, which they may not understand. They are homesick and don't understand why you sent them away. Parents will feel guilty that they have admitted their child and that they couldn't fix this by themselves, but they are also relieved that the decision was finally made and that help is on the way. All of these feelings are normal. You are not a bad parent simply because you made a decision to ask for help, and many times this kind of help requires inpatient care for the health and safety of the child. As a parent, caregiver, or support provider, you take the risk that the unknown hospital variables will not outweigh the benefits of admitting the child. Hospitalization should never be used as a threat to motivate a child to behave more appropriately. If and when the child ever needs this kind of intervention, he or she (and you) should know for sure that these facilities and the people who work in them will only help the child and not hurt him or her.

A good way to "predict" this possible decision for your child would be to say, "We're going to do everything we can to help you control yourself at home, but in case we are not able to, there are places where we can get help. These are hospitals that have people who are specially trained to work with children who are having a hard time." I gave Zachary this information about a month prior to hospitalization, when I knew it was a possibility.

6

Repetitive Thoughts and Behaviors: When Your Child Can't Stop Thinking about Vacuums or Similar Objects

Obsessions and compulsions are core features of Asperger's syndrome. These symptoms can be quite disabling at times.

Medical Perspective

The characteristics or nuances of obsessive-compulsive disorder (OCD) in Asperger's syndrome are unique. There are fewer obsessive thoughts of checking and cleaning behavior in Asperger's OCD, but there are more compulsive acts of repeating, hoarding, touching, tapping, and self-damaging behaviors. At times these can take the form of severe rituals and self-injurious behavior.

The incidence of obsessions and compulsions in Asperger's syndrome can be quite high; some studies have found OCD in 30 to 40 percent of children diagnosed with Asperger's syndrome. The symptoms are frequently treatment-resistant and can offer unique challenges. The best practice of treatment for OCD is cognitive-behavioral therapy (CBT)—behavior modification that consists of closely monitored response prevention—in conjunction with medication. Therapists usually need to combine the two interventions. Unfortunately, we don't have enough professionals who can effectively implement these strategies. There are not enough people who have trained adequately in cognitive-behavioral therapy attuned to the special needs in Asperger's syndrome.

The next section focuses on the pharmacological interventions that have been found to be useful in the management of the behaviors.

Medical Intervention

SSRIs, or antidepressant drugs, are one of the main pharmacological agents for the treatment of OCD comorbid with Asperger's syndrome. These drugs increase the chemical serotonin in some of the key areas of the brain—namely, the basal ganglia and the hippocampus. The benefits of the medication are achieved only by progressively increasing the dosage.

The SSRIs Prozac (fluoxetine), Zoloft (sertraline), and Luvox (fluoxamine) may help in controlling obsessive thoughts and compulsive behaviors and are FDA-approved for OCD treatment in children and adolescents. In addition, Anafranil (clomipramine), an older medication, has been quite successful in controlling OCD behaviors and is considered the gold standard. However, it has many side effects, and an electrocardiogram (EKG) must be done regularly to monitor the heart. The dosage must be increased very slowly. As long as the doctor is practicing due diligence, however, it's a very useful drug.

The SSRIs are by and large safe and have a similar risk for suicidality irrespective of dosage. We practice caution and are very diligent in the first ten days and then the first thirty days when most of this effect takes place. The vulnerable population is children and adults up to twenty-five years old. SSRIs are effective in treating many OCD symptoms, in conjunction with relieving anxiety and mood issues, which are frequently diagnosed in these children. One placebo-controlled trial suggested the benefit of Prozac (fluoxetine) in treating children with generalized anxiety and social anxiety disorder. Zoloft (sertraline) has also shown its efficacy in the treatment of obsessive-compulsive symptoms. In addition, useful data are emerging on the benefits of Celexa (citalopram) and Lexapro (escitalopram).

The primary recommendation is to start any medication at a very low dose. Take Zoloft (sertraline) as an example. It is my (Syed's) practice to start with half of a 25 mg tablet for the first seven days and then increase slowly and gradually to a whole 25 mg tablet. I monitor the effectiveness and then, in six to eight weeks, depending on the clinical response, adjust the medication slowly until it is at an ideal dosage. These medications take eight to ten weeks to show any benefits, so practitioners and caregivers should resist making quick changes in medications based on slow or no apparent positive results. It takes time to see if a medication works.

Medication usage in OCD frequently requires higher dosages and must be monitored closely for side effects. The main side effects of these medications are dry mouth, drowsiness, neck spasm, abdominal discomfort, and restlessness. However, most of these side effects tend to be transitory, lasting for only a few days. Occasionally there is a mild agitation and a lack of acceptance in the child toward the medication in the first ten days. Parents and caregivers need to be educated and trained to ride out this brief storm for the larger overall good of the child. This side effect is seen mostly with Prozac (fluoxetine) and can be reduced by starting the medication in very low doses and concentrations.

Serious side effects occur rarely, such as agitation, lack of sleep, abnormal euphoria, severe anxiety, and, very rarely, suicidal ideation.

Serious side effects, including thoughts of self-harm, usually but not always occur in the first ten to thirty days of starting treatment. Many of them can be avoided by starting with a low dosage and moving slowly toward an optimal dose. I insist on and expect communication from the parent, highlighting the absence of these side effects via phone, email, or faxed letter, approximately two weeks after starting pharmacological treatment. This helps to catch the problem at the beginning, before it has a chance to turn into a full-blown crisis. The emergence of rare but serious side effects requires controlled discontinuation of the medication; that is, the medications cannot be stopped abruptly. Children must remain under the care of an experienced practitioner during the discontinuation of a medication.

Following are the recommended starting dosages and their clinical range in treating obsessive-compulsive symptoms in Asperger's syndrome:

- **Celexa (citalopram):** Starting dose, 10 mg. In children younger than eight years of age, 5 mg. Average dose, 20–40 mg. Maximum dose, 60 mg.
- **Prozac (fluoxetine):** Starting dose, 5 mg. Average dose, 30–40 mg. Maximum dose, 80 mg.
- **Luvox (fluoxamine):** Starting dose, 25 mg. Average dose, 200 mg. Maximum dose, 250 mg.
- **Zoloft (sertraline):** Starting dose, 25 mg. Average dose, 100–125 mg. Maximum dose, 200 mg.
- **Anafranil (clomipramine):** This is used in cases in which SSRIs have not adequately treated the symptoms. This is an

old medication in the tricyclic class of antidepressants, and it has a significant effect on the serotonin in the brain. The usual starting dose is half of a 25 mg tablet, gradually increasing to 50 to 100 mg. Do not increase the dose more rapidly than 25 mg at a time. It has some major side effects: it can cause rapid heart rate and prolongation of EKG intervals. Therefore, children who are using this medication need to be closely monitored. The overall treatment regimen with anafranil may take up to eight to twelve weeks to determine its efficacy and other clinical responses. If your child complains of heart palpitations or feeling jittery, your physician should be contacted immediately. One must continually weigh the benefits of the medication against the potential and current side effects.

Sometimes children do not respond to a particular drug. When a primary medication has not proved to be helpful, another medication may be added. This is called an *augmentation strategy*. An augmentation strategy is used to enhance the effectiveness of a medication. You first increase the dosage then usually augment based on response. If there is at least a 50 percent response, then you do not want to lose the gains and will want to augment. Medication is changed if the response is less than 40 percent to 50 percent. The most frequently used drugs for this strategy are a new class called atypical antipsychotic medications. These are used in very low dosages and only in addition to the primary medication.

The FDA recently approved an antipsychotic medication called Risperdal (risperidone) for autistic or Asperger's symptoms, and it remains the most frequently used and beneficial of the group. Abilify (aripiprazole), Geodon (ziprasidone), and Zyprexa (olanzapine) are the other drugs in this group. Risperdal is used in the lowest possible dose: 0.25–0.5 mg.

All of the above medications have been shown to alleviate symptoms of obsessions and compulsions, however, not without possible, though rare, significant side effects of abnormal thoughts and psychosis.

It is difficult to know exactly how long a medication should be continued. Many of the patients with OCD symptoms in Asperger's syndrome have a waxing and waning of symptoms. Treatment is usually continued for a year and a half to two years. It is my practice to give a trial without medication by slowly tapering off the medication in this length of time. However, very few children can successfully be tapered off. In the case of relapse, it is not uncommon to reinstitute medication treatment. There are no clear data on these results and responses, and the clinician along with the family has to make rational and informed treatment decisions. This requires a clear perspective of long-term growth and development of the child.

Children may be reluctant to take medication when side effects become prominent or because it is not part of their routine. This requires a gentle handling by the adults involved. Medications require a team approach with appropriate behavioral therapy.

Home-to-School Perspective

The Diagnostic and Statistical Manual of Mental Disorders (DSM-IV) describes the symptoms of OCD as recurring thoughts that are intrusive and inappropriate and cause great anxiety and distress. These thoughts and impulses are not about real-life problems. People with this disorder attempt to ignore or suppress the thoughts, or to neutralize them in some other manner, but cannot. At first the person might believe that the thoughts are imposed by some external source, but eventually he or she recognizes that the thoughts are in his or her own mind. People with this disorder also realize that the obsessions or compulsions are unreasonable and excessive.

For instance, a person might be completely consumed with the thought of germs, getting sick, and needing to wash off the germs and thus be unable to attend to normal daily activities unless the thoughts are neutralized in some way. This is the obsession.

The only way that the person feels "right" or "normal" is to wash his or her hands over and over. That is the compulsion.

The DSM-IV states that people with Asperger's syndrome engage in a stereotyped or repetitive use of language; this description assumes, of course, that the child is verbal. If the child is not verbal, then this stereotyped use of "language" manifests itself in extraordinarily repetitive behaviors such as spinning wheels or lining up blocks over and over.

The main difference between true OCD and the repetitive thoughts and behaviors of Asperger's syndrome is that people with true OCD are able to eventually acknowledge that the thoughts are not caused by an external variable and therefore are able to recognize its intrusiveness. This awareness allows the individual to actively participate in the road to recovery, using such interventions as cognitive-behavioral therapy. In Asperger's syndrome, the awareness is missing, and our children would engage in their repetitive thoughts and behaviors all day long if we let them, which makes it very difficult for them to participate in their treatment.

It takes significant intervention, constant monitoring of conversations and social skills, and an environmental awareness for a child to understand that his or her thoughts or behaviors require some boundaries. Most of the time, our children do not come to this realization on their own and ask for help. That is where you and/or your physician come in.

Everyone Has Hobbies; How Is This Different?

I (Melinda) can't begin to count the amount of times I have been asked this question by parents, teachers, and other professionals. Their biggest concern is that I am possibly not allowing my son to engage in and pursue his choice of interests. As caregivers in all capacities, they are also concerned that they might miss noticing that a child needs intervention. I can assure you that not noticing a child who truly needs intervention due to repetitive thoughts and behaviors is not possible. As a parent, I have witnessed a wide range of obsessions, both unusual and mainstream; some have lasted for a week, others for a year. I have learned more than I ever wanted to know about adhesive tape, Whoville from *How the Grinch Stole Christmas!*, and journals, date books, and day planners, to name just a few.

My answer to the question "How do you really know?" is this. When your child is waking you at 5:30 on a Saturday morning to ask you how many pages were in the journal that you both saw on Wednesday at the store, it is time to intervene. When your child's interests are disruptive to social, emotional, and academic growth and to family involvement and sibling and peer relationships, then it is time to intervene, regardless of a name, label, or diagnosis. It is your job to facilitate your child's interests with parental encouragement while also teaching him or her to realize that not everyone is interested in the same thing.

Exceptional Knowledge or True Disruption?

How many of you were absolutely sure, without a doubt, that your child was a genius, based on knowledge of unusual topics, memorization skills well beyond his or her years, and attention to detail at a very young age? My hand is raised with yours. It stayed raised until my son said to me one day, "The other kids—they don't like journals as much as I do, do they?"

"No, they don't," I replied.

"How do I get my brain to stop thinking about journals and start thinking about Pokémon?" Zachary asked. "Just tell me what to do, and I'll do whatever you say."

In many ways, this child *is* a genius, with a wide range of knowledge, facts, and details about many subjects, many of which I know nothing about. I in no way wanted to take that skill and expertise from him. I just wanted him to eventually be able to control it and guide it into something that would build his self-esteem and benefit him in some way, not leave him feeling as though he had no other choices but to succumb to the thoughts. If you are fortunate enough to have a child who can articulate the inability to control obsessive thoughts, such as by saying, "Mommy, I just want to play with the other kids at recess, but I can't stop my brain from thinking, so I have to tell them no," then you are one of the lucky few. If you are like many parents I know, whose children are so enthralled with their own conversations about vacuum cleaners, then you have to intervene.

Imaginative Play or Exact Replica?

You want nothing more than to see your six-year-old playing with a friend in the schoolyard, and finally you do, but then you realize that he or she is only mimicking what the other kids are doing, not actually interacting with them.

Perhaps he or she has simply re-created a scene, such as a visit to the dentist's office, in your living room. Imaginative play, either alone or with others, does include replicating a scene or event. However, there usually is some flexibility in the conversations taking place in this imaginative play. For example, re-creating a visit to the dentist would include the doctor and the equipment as well as acting as though someone is the patient. Imaginative play also includes the child putting him- or herself in the shoes of one of the characters but also taking on the role and using their own personality. When playing with another child, it would also include allowing the peer to interpret the game in his or her own way. This is imaginative play.

Exact replication would include the child using the actual words the doctor used without any flexibility in intonation, sentence structure, or wording. In other words, the scene would be played out exactly as it happened, and if anything differed from the original, the child with Asperger's syndrome would become anxious and upset that it wasn't correct.

I remember observing a child with Asperger's syndrome in a first-grade class. I wanted to observe social interaction. What better time than recess, I thought; it's a completely unstructured free-for-all. All the boys were playing tag, and the boy I was watching was playing with them—or so it seemed, at first glance. The game of tag involves running, screaming, touching, and yelling "*It!*" The student I was watching was engaging in all the appropriate behaviors. He was running, screaming, tagging, and yelling "*It!*" Then suddenly the group of boys decided that they didn't want to play anymore. This student then decided to play house with the girls. Unfortunately, the rules of playing house are not running, screaming, tagging, and yelling "*It!*" The student attempted to take the rules he learned for tag and apply them to all outside games, including playing house.

Home-to-School Interventions

Throughout the years, I have found many strategies that have worked for my son and the students I work with in my professional life. The strategies are not easy, and they take much patience and consistency, on the part of both the child and yourself.

Setting Boundaries

There is a fine line between encouraging an interest and enabling an obsession. Finding this delicate balance is of the utmost importance. As a mother, I wanted to buy my son many, many journals. As a mother, I wanted him to stop asking strangers to see their date books. As a mother, I wanted others to understand and forgive. As a professional, I knew they wouldn't and they shouldn't.

Therefore, I allowed Zachary to write in his journals for a reasonable amount of time. He was allowed to ask only Mom, Dad, Grandma, and Grandpa to see their date books. He was not allowed to ask anyone else. He was told that date books are private materials but that others might allow him to see them because they don't want to say no. We would help him to monitor the behavior until he could monitor it for himself.

Zachary understood. The rule was concrete, clear, and easy to follow. In addition, time limits were set on Zachary's ongoing monologue about the obsession. This probably won't feel right to you, as a parent. We feel most comfortable encouraging our children to share their interests as much and as often as possible. However, please remember: every time your child engages in a topic of conversation beyond what would be considered a reasonable amount of time, that is time that he or she is not gaining other skills, such as initiating play, interacting with peers, and learning about his or her environment. As difficult as it was, and as unfair as it seemed to my son, it is what I found to be best for him, in the long run.

Never punish a child by taking away career-related activities, says Dr. Temple Grandin. Talents should be nurtured. Art supplies should never be taken away from a budding artist or computer use from a potential programmer.

Using the Obsession as a Motivator

Whether you are a parent, a teacher, a therapist, or a caregiver, it would be most beneficial for you to understand that even though you might be able to get a child to stop *talking* about an obsessive interest, the chances are that no matter how wonderful you are at what you do, you will not get the child to stop *thinking* about it. Here is a perfect example of teaching and learning through perspective. Our ideal is for the child to be able to control his or her thoughts in order to think about other things, do other things, and interact with others. However, that is not what the child has in store for you at this time.

Therefore, you will have to intervene (academically, socially, or otherwise), keeping in mind that this child would rather think about black holes. I once asked my son if he could choose to listen to the teacher rather than think about journals. His reply was enlightening: "Why would I ever do that?" You must use the child's interest in your favor. For instance, say, "Do three math problems, then you can talk about vacuums for one minute," or "Ask your sister if she wants to share your toy, then you can color a picture of a vacuum cleaner."

This is very simplified, but you get the idea. Teachers will have to use the child's obsessive thoughts as a motivator. The key is to provide your expertise and intervention within the boundaries of the child's perception. If that perception is that nothing is more important than vacuum cleaners, then that is what you have to work with. If you are not willing to relinquish control in this manner, then you will be fighting a losing battle—and no math problems will ever be completed!

Encouraging Mainstream Interests

Many of the child's interests will be of a highly unusual nature. However, every once in a while, and hopefully more often than not, the child's intense interest will be mainstream enough that it will provide the perfect friend-making opportunities.

What do you do if your child remains interested only in journals? You must be creative enough to find something that will connect your child to the mainstream population through that interest. For instance, there is a series of Harry Potter journals. Perhaps you can move your child from an interest in journals to an interest in the Harry Potter books, which are a current mainstream interest. It might be that the only thing written in those journals will be drawings of vacuum cleaners, but it's a step, and you can take only one step at a time.

Create opportunities for the child to have age-appropriate peer discussions on common interests. This includes playdates, park visits, and activities in school that would include these interests. This might be a good way for a parent to volunteer in the classroom and plan an activity that could include their child's interest but involve all of the children in the classroom.

Turning to Medication

I am not going to advocate or dispute medication here; I merely want to present it as another viable option for intervention. From a personal point of view, I can tell you that my son could not function, nor would he have gained the skills and successes that he has, without it.

My advice in this area is to do your homework. Research any and all possible medications, side effects, and interactions. Read the published clinical studies on the particular medication that you are considering. You know your child better than anyone. Search for a physician, if that is the route you decide to take, with whom both you and your child feel comfortable. If you know that you are an anxious parent, as I am, find someone who will embrace that and who can reassure you, not make you feel like a burden. Only then will you calm down.

Most important, be very specific when you describe your child's symptoms and challenges to the physician. I can't tell you how many children I have worked with whose physicians have put them on stimulants simply because the parents said they could not pay attention, when in fact they couldn't pay attention because they had obsessions, not because their external environment was overstimulating.

Current research supports that combined therapies are more effective than medication alone. A 2009 article in the *Journal of the American Academy of Child and Adolescent Psychiatry* showed that medication and behavioral treatment was more effective than medication alone.

7

Theory of Mind: How to Walk in My Shoes

Early psychological studies of Asperger's syndrome focused on attention, memory, and metacognitive processes. *Theory of mind*—the ability to know another person's beliefs and desires and to use that knowledge to predict future behavior—is a core concept that has evolved in the past two decades in understanding the challenges of Asperger's syndrome.

Medical Perspective

Pioneer work done by Simon Baron-Cohen from 1985 to 2000 has shown that Asperger's syndrome is a specific cognitive disorder of mental blindness, an inability to interpret nonverbal cues and make inferences from those cues. Theory of mind, or mentalizing ability, was examined by using tests of false beliefs. The person with Asperger's syndrome acts on the basis of his or her own beliefs rather than on the basis of how things really are.

Deficits in theory of mind have been found in individuals with Asperger's syndrome through many experimental protocols. Up to 50 percent of individuals failed the first-order theory of mind test. This can be simply explained in terms of lack or deficit of empathy and is best described as an inability to walk in someone else's shoes.

The social difficulty associated with theory of mind in Asperger's syndrome is based on not understanding what another person is thinking. This has been attributed to impairments in general cognitive processes. It is believed that a deficit in theory of mind impairs attention, memory, and day-to-day executive functioning. Studies have shown that executive functioning, or the ability to thoughtfully plan out a sequence of daily activities and implement those activities, in Asperger's is based on false beliefs.

Theory of mind occurs as a deficit in a variety of disabilities in addition to Asperger's syndrome, including mental retardation and severe language impairment. In Asperger's syndrome, theory of mind appears to be specifically related to language-based strategies. A majority of social and nonverbal communication abilities in young children with Asperger's syndrome are also evident in individuals who have severe language impairment but not Asperger's syndrome. This tells us that language is integrally related to the concept of theory of mind.

Theory of mind also affects one's ability to follow another person's gaze, to point and show a peer something of interest, and to be present in the here and now. Sometimes deficits in these areas are confused with ADHD, because the child appears to be inattentive; however, inattentiveness due to autistic symptoms is very different from inattentiveness due to ADHD.

In a scientific study, R. Hobson, C. Peterson, and M. Siegel studied blind children and found that children with visual impairment use alternative cognitive strategies to achieve social competence. The children with visual impairments were able to compensate for their visual disability and form relationships using other strategies, whereas children with Asperger's syndrome were not.

Asperger's Syndrome and Criminality

There is a great deal of controversy related to the issue of Asperger's syndrome and the committing of criminal offenses. Although the press has reported a tentative relationship between Asperger's syndrome and criminal activity, research in Michigan by a group of child and adolescent psychiatrists has clearly shown that individuals with Asperger's syndrome do not necessarily commit crimes. The majority of these individuals live within the framework of the law.

One of the common issues faced by children with Asperger's syndrome is teasing and bullying by others at a young age. Past injustices can become concrete in the minds of these individuals, and at times this will lead to bizarre forms of retribution. Some of the situations may have taken place decades earlier, but the desire for revenge remains in the forefront of the individual's mind, causing the retribution to come at a much later date, which makes the violent act appear to have come out of nowhere. Thus the relationship between the past bullying and the act of retribution is not always seen, which in many cases causes an incorrect assumptions.

Furthermore, because of the desire for peer acceptance, many individuals with Asperger's syndrome have been found to have been set up by their colleagues to commit acts of criminality or to be dared into committing acts of violence, and that has sometimes led to tremendous problems. There is some debate about the existence of a malicious subgroup of Asperger's individuals who do engage in acts of harm toward others.

Hans Asperger coined the term *autistic malice* in one of his cases. My (Syed's) clinical experience has not found these traits in Asperger's patients. However, because of the lack of affective reciprocity, social competence, and shrewdness or guile in many Asperger's individuals, boys may appear to be little dictators and use nuances of violence, and girls may use emotional blackmail to gain power and control in social situations. This has led to society's perception of a higher instance of criminality.

Sometimes individuals with Asperger's syndrome simply display behaviors that are a public nuisance. This can manifest itself in sexually inappropriate behavior, which is not, however, sexually abusive or sexually violent behavior. The lack of theory of mind can make it difficult for these individuals to differentiate between kindness and attraction. A friendly act by another may be presumed by the individual with the disorder to be a romantic or sexual overture, therefore resulting in an inappropriate response by the person with Asperger's syndrome.

A focus on isolated sexual pleasure can be observed in many of these individuals, because they have not had the usual social range of sexual experiences. Because of their lack of sexual experience, they may develop sexual arousal and fantasies in conjunction with disturbing paraphilias, such as compulsive masturbation, addiction to pornography, and sex that is more rote than meaningful. Pathological fantasies are addressed in cognitive-behavioral therapy utilizing exposure and response prevention. This remains a challenge, but the approach is to catch the paraphilias early, to bring about relief in a structured format with guidance, and to increase appropriate socialization through social skills training and social skills groups.

Medical Intervention

The use of low doses of atypical antipsychotic agents like risperidone has shown some mixed results in the improvement of theory of mind. I am not convinced that the effects are long-term and beneficial overall. The risk-benefit ratio behooves us to be cautious in the use of these agents. The improvement appears to be more in thought process and thought content than in the fundamental deficits in theory of mind.

Home-to-School Perspective

There are many definitions of theory of mind. It is most commonly considered to be a specific cognitive capacity that involves the ability to attribute mental state, desire, and knowledge to oneself and to others, understanding that others' beliefs, desires, and intentions are different from one's own.

A simple definition is that theory of mind is the ability to put yourself in someone else's shoes. It is an understanding that others will be influenced by what you say and what you do. Theory of mind is the ability to understand that someone else may have a perception or a feeling that you do not have about an identical situation.

Sympathy is different from empathy. A sympathetic person is able to understand what someone else is going through; an empathic person not only understands the situation but actually feels as if he or she is the other person who is directly experiencing that situation.

Empathy: Can You Teach It?

I have had many parents ask me if empathy can be taught. Without a doubt, you can teach children to *respond* in empathetic ways in situations. However, can you teach a child to express empathy because he or she is actually *feeling* it rather than because he or she has simply *learned* it? That is a question that I cannot answer. Ideally, we want our children to respond with empathy because they feel it, but I do not know if all of our children will eventually get there.

Recall the example I (Melinda) cited in an earlier chapter. When Zachary was very young, my daughter pulled a chair over on top of herself, and even though she was fine, she was crying. Rather walking over to her and saying, "Are you okay, do you need any help?", Zachary responded by saying to me, "She is making too much noise; take her out of the room." In order to learn empathy, he had to be given a social script.

Social Scripts

Zachary was given the following instruction: when you see your sister crying, your choices are to say "Are you okay?" or to ask an adult for help. These choices, though specific to this particular situation, generalize quite often to school and other social environments. When our children witness someone falling on the playground, we do not want them to say, "Hey, move out of my way." That does not help children to make and keep friends or to grow up to be caring adults.

Zachary was taught how to compliment people, how to ask about someone's well-being, and how to apologize. It took quite a few years before it became natural to him and before he understood that many of the scripts can be generalized to similar situations in other environments. He also had to be taught to make eye contact with the person to whom he was speaking rather than with the adult who was prompting him to engage in the appropriate behavior. In other words, if I was saying to him, "You need to say you are sorry to your sister" or "You need to ask your sister if she needs some help," he also had to be prompted to look at his sister rather than at me even though I was the one speaking to him.

Nonverbal Cues

Many, if not all, of the social scripts taught to children with Asperger's syndrome should include nonverbal rules. We learn a great deal about others from their nonverbal cues, such as eye movements, facial expressions, and hand gestures. A smile, a frown, eye contact, or eye avoidance communicate a lot, sometimes reinforcing and sometimes belying the words we are speaking. I have used many strategies to teach this. At times, I use actual photographs of children to point out frowns, anger, happiness, sadness, and worry. These nonverbal expressions have to be taught with the concreteness of teaching someone to play the piano. For example, one might say, "When the lips are turned up, that means a smile," or "When you see someone with tears, that might mean they are upset and you can ask them if they need help or if something is wrong." Another example would be teach the child with Asperger's that if the peer they are talking to "rolls their eyes" (you must show them what this looks like) or turns their body away that might mean they aren't interested in what you have to say or they want to change the conversation.

Each of these nonverbal descriptions must be accompanied by a script that the child can use, or they are of no use. A typical child will interpret these nonverbal cues and respond accordingly. Children with Asperger's syndrome can determine the meaning of the nonverbal cues by use of memorization and practice and then implement the social script and response that they have been taught. Ideally, they will eventually be able to identify similar situations and utilize the scripts across a variety of environments.

Home-to-School Interventions

Zachary needed to be taught what kind of message a person's eyes communicated, what a facial gesture meant in a particular situation, what it meant to be ignored, and how to respond.

The Monitoring of Social Interactions

Constant monitoring of social interactions was a must. It is very difficult for Asperger's children to understand that they must behave in an appropriate manner in a particular situation and to utilize a particular script if it is not monitored and consistently reinforced every time a similar situation comes up. Ideally, we would like the child to eventually recognize the similarities between several similar situations and their possible script choices.

I am happy to say that this constant monitoring is no longer necessary with Zachary. A parent's next question might be, "Is it because he now understands social interactions or because he has a variety of social scripts in his head that are available to him in many situations?" My response is, "Does it matter?"

Yes, ideally it would be nice to know that our children have learned theory of mind so well that it has become second nature for them, but if not, the next best thing is to teach them to respond and interact appropriately. In my son's case, I do believe that he truly understands the idiosyncrasies of nonverbal language; however, that is not true for all kids.

Where Are the Shortcuts?

I once sat in on a psychiatric conference. It was quite a few years ago, before many psychiatrists were treating or diagnosing children with Asperger's syndrome. It was right about the time that the DSM-IV, which included Asperger's syndrome, had been published. The majority of psychiatrists at this conference treated adults and were therefore unfamiliar with diagnosis, early intervention, and clinical symptoms for children. One person asked about the "shortcuts" in intervention. There are no shortcuts.

Theory of mind takes many years to develop. The only way to implement any sort of intervention for theory of mind is to constantly have someone with the children, prompting them, having them refer back to similar situations, explaining why they are similar, and then using social scripts and social stories to indicate the options for responding in a particular situation. A child needs a clear understanding of how to respond to another child in a particular situation. This is achieved by clear indications and clear instructions on choices of social scripts. Unfortunately, there are no shortcuts. Progress is long-term, and success is determined by the child's ability to make a connection with the skill that is taught to the situation in which it should be applied. Success is also directly related to the consistency of the adult monitoring the conversations and interactions and their willingness to continue these interventions on a daily basis for many years. I started this when Zachary was about two. Third grade was when I started to notice the success. Progress happened all along, but it was not until he was about eight that I started to see the difference. As you might imagine, this would be very difficult for a teacher to monitor on a daily basis with thirty other students, or a therapist to intervene once a week. This supports the fact that parents have to be involved and all team members need to be implementing the same intervention, using the same scripts.

The Generalization of Skills

A child has just dropped her lunch tray. The choices of a child with Asperger's syndrome are to help her clean up, offer words of encouragement, or ask an adult for help. Another child is upset because he has lost a baseball game. The Asperger's child may be taught to say, "I know it's tough to lose sometimes" or "Nice try; better luck next time." This option is then used in other situations in which a child might not have a desired outcome, such as an art contest or a math test, and the responses can be used in the same way.

However, keep in mind that the social responses must be appropriate to the lingo used by the particular age group. Otherwise it will not be appropriate. For example; a boy in middle school may be taught to initiate conversation with others by saying, "Hey, how's it going?" or "Whatcha up to?" or "How was your weekend?" These would be very appropriate conversation starters with his peers, but not to initiate a conversation with me.

After many years of practice with intervention provided consistently on a daily basis, the child might eventually be able to recognize similar situations and generalize the skill and social script to that new situation. This takes a great deal of practice and consistency by the adult to make the child aware that this situation is just like the other one. For example, the child learned to ask his neighbor Jane if she wants to play. He learned to script, "Hi Jane, do you want to play ball?" If he has generalized this skill, he will be able to use a similar script when he is with Mark and be able to say "Hi Mark, do you want to play video games?" If he has not learned to generalize, then he will use the "Jane" script with Mark.

8

ADHD and Executive Function: Putting Your Thoughts in Order

Before we go into the treatment modalities that are available for hyperkinesis (increased and sometimes uncontrollable muscular movements), inattentiveness, and impulsivity in Asperger's syndrome, it is important to clarify the constellation of symptomatology that we see in Asperger's syndrome.

Medical Perspective

Attentional issues in children with Asperger's syndrome are due not necessarily to a deficit in attention or the ability to focus but to a deficit in the ability to listen to a set of instructions and either recall the content or implement the steps of the directions in the order necessary to complete the task. The lack of close attention to details and to the completion of ordinary tasks—common characteristics of ADHD—are different with Asperger's syndrome.

Distractibility is a characteristic of ADHD but not of Asperger's syndrome. In a child with Asperger's syndrome, we may see an innate incapacity to attend to a task. This can be observed as a lack of eye contact and may be due to lack of motivation. However, it would be a mistake to confuse these phenomena with distractibility. Completing a task can be independently challenging in Asperger's syndrome as well, but not because of distractibility.

Hyperkinesis in ADHD manifests as impulsiveness and overactivity. This is sometimes confused with stereotactic, or repetitive rote, movements, which are perhaps more related to anxiety. Impulsiveness means acting without any appropriate reflection or forethought.

It can be extremely difficult to differentiate between autism spectrum disorder and ADHD, especially the form of autism known as Asperger's syndrome. There are several reasons. First, the behavioral patterns of both show similar etiological factors, such as diffuse brain disorder with biological underpinnings.

Second, a child with autism can demonstrate motor restlessness such as fidgeting, pacing, and hand movements due to perseveration with idiosyncratic movement patterns. In ADHD, the hyperactivity is global and does not seem to have a pattern attached to it. The same kind of impulsiveness can be very specific in Asperger's syndrome, but in ADHD it can be global and nonrelated or nonsequential.

The third and the most important issue in autism spectrum disorder is that hyperactivity, hyperkinesis, impulsivity, and inattention can be a manifestation or a side effect of the drugs that are used to treat many of the symptoms of Asperger's syndrome. For example, the use of atypical antipsychotic medications to treat aggression or irritability in Asperger's syndrome can sometimes lead to cognitive dullness, cognitive decline, and cognitive slowness, which can all be mistaken for inattentiveness. This presents unique challenges in the management of the symptoms.

Medical Intervention

Medication treatment for ADHD symptoms in Asperger's syndrome differs based on IQ. For children with an IQ higher than 50, the treatment matches the normal ADHD protocol.

Stimulants like Dexedrine (dextroamphetamine), Ritalin (methylphenidate), Adderall (mixed amphetamine salts), and Strattera (atomoxetine hydrochloride) are the main drugs used. Children with an IQ above 50 have a more positive response rate with stimulants, but the response can vary in children with an IQ below 50. Stimulants can make these children even more hyperactive, impulsive, and aggressive than they already were (which was what mandated treatment in the first place). They therefore require vigilant monitoring.

Stimulants have not been found to be consistently useful in the treatment of hyperactivity in children with Asperger's syndrome. Overall, the response rate in autism spectrum disorder is approximately 35 to 40 percent, compared to 70 percent in classic ADHD (no diagnosis of Asperger's syndrome).

Stimulants come with potentially significant side effects. Stunted growth, weight loss, appetite suppression, sleep disturbance, exacerbation of anxiety, and an increase in irritability are all possible side effects that must be very closely monitored and managed.

Most stimulants require a baseline blood test and liver function tests. An awareness of drug interactions is also essential, since many of these children are on more than one medication.

It is also advisable to monitor children with a history of heart disease, using an EKG in addition to monitoring the rhythm of the heart. It is necessary to exercise special caution with minority children and with children and adults from different ethnic backgrounds, due to complications of drug interactions.

Response and efficacy of different medications can vary based on one's genetic and gender makeup. For example, you can be a slow or a rapid metabolizer of a specific medication based on your genetic constitution and an innate biological ability to metabolize and eliminate the medications from your body.

Some stimulants can produce effects in doses much lower than what is recommended.

There is increasing evidence of the effectiveness of Strattera (atomoxetine) in treating inattentiveness, impulsivity, and hyperactivity in children with both Asperger's syndrome and ADHD. However, there is also evidence of children on Strattera engaging in self-harm and even suicide, which has led to a black-box warning by the FDA. Children on this drug must be monitored carefully. Strattera can also cause an activation syndrome (increased agitation, severe anxiety, and severe mood lability) and manic behavior.

Two classic antihypertensive medications, Catapres (clonidine) and Tenex (guanfacine), are also used in Asperger's syndrome. Tenex is longer-acting, whereas Catapres tends to be shorter-acting. They work in specific areas of the brain to reduce impulsivity and hyperactivity. However, they don't appear to be especially effective with inattentiveness. Their side effects seem to be limited to tiredness and a drop in blood pressure, both of which are benign. In November 2009 an extended-release form of guanfacine, Intuniv, was launched and has shown good initial clinical results in managing ADHD symptomatology, specifically in managing the hyperactive impulsive component. Intuniv is a slow-release formulation of Tenex and has shown promising initial results in children with Asperger's disorder who have severe issues around impulsive/hyperactive behavior.

Besides stimulants and antihypertensives, two other types of medications have occasionally been used off-label to treat the ADHD-like symptoms of Asperger's syndrome: Wellbutrin (bupropion), which is an antidepressant, and Provigil (modafinil), which is used to treat excessive sleepiness (such as narcolepsy). I do not recommend the use of Provigil off-label by and large, but it is used if other standard meds are not working. It is a useful med if used with caution and with a clear understanding of the risk for rash and its possible lethality.

Home-to-School Perspective

How do we as educators and parents decide when impulsive behavior, such as talking out of turn, should be labeled pathological and treated with what are often very dangerous drugs? When should it be considered a psychiatric disease for a child to be fidgety and not be able to sit still in a classroom (perhaps because he or she is bored) and having difficulty prioritizing?

It is difficult but not impossible to make these distinctions. Many clinicians will say that students with Asperger's syndrome can also have ADHD. There are just as many who will argue that attentional issues (beyond what is well within the range of normal behavior) are part and parcel of Asperger's syndrome itself. In order to discern the difference—and yes, you do have to differentiate, especially if you are going to use medication as an intervention—you have to determine the etiology, or fundamental basis, of the attentional issues.

Are they due to external stimuli, something about the classroom environment, such as noise, peer activity, students talking all at once, the air conditioning turning on, or the desk being filled with all sorts of extraneous accessories that are not required for school? Or is the lack of attention due to a child's active imagination? Are the children creating pictures or stories in their heads that they find much more interesting and motivating than whatever the teacher is saying?

The Organization of Thoughts

Children with Asperger's syndrome continue to struggle with what is called *executive function*, a term used to describe the skills that are necessary to become a responsible, well-functioning adult. These skills include planning ability, working memory, impulse control, and inhibition. When children have trouble with these skills, is it because they are distracted by external stimuli, because they are distracted by their thoughts, or because they have trouble with the organization of their thoughts?

Executive function is the ability to organize your thoughts, to put them in order and be able to plan your way through an activity so you can turn your thoughts into actions. For example, if I (Melinda) am giving a lecture to a group of adults and I ask them to turn to page 23 in their books, I would expect them to be able to do so. I would not expect to have to tell them to look down at the bottom right-hand corner of the right-hand page for the page number, take their right hand, hold the top corner of the right side of that page, turn it, and keep doing this until they come to page 23. This is a skill that the general population, or those considered "neurotypical," have learned from their natural environment. Most of us learned this skill at a very young age, and it is something we take for granted. However, this skill, and others like it, are extremely difficult for many of our children.

Information Processing

At one point I was asked to come in to a kindergarten class and observe a boy who had been diagnosed with Asperger's syndrome. I arrived in the classroom just as the teacher was finishing reading-circle time. Her instructions were as follows: "Go back to your seats and take out your math books." It seemed like a simple enough direction, and for most of the children, it was.

However, for this little boy, the teacher might as well have been speaking a foreign language. I watched all the other children walk to their seats, put their books in their desks, get out their math books, and sit down. This boy, however, went to his desk, realized that the desk was a mess, and did not know what to do, because, since he was holding a book, he had no free hands with which to clean up his desk, much less get out his math book.

It became very apparent to me that this child realized that the required action was to take out his math book, but he was not able to process the steps that were required to achieve this end. As he stood there, all eyes upon him, the teacher continued to say to him, "What did I tell you to do? What are you supposed to be doing?" and the child just looked at her, his anxiety increasing with every passing moment. Unfortunately the teacher did not model her request; she simply did the task for him, telling him to listen next time.

Task Analysis

Because children with Asperger's syndrome have so much trouble with following anything more complex than two-step directions, we have to task-analyze activities, which means that we break instructions into several parts and then check for understanding after one part before we give the next part.

In the above example, what we thought was a two-step direction—"Go back to your seats and take out your math books"—turns out to have been a seven-step direction for this child. The directions for this child should have been "Johnny, please get up; now walk to your desk; put down your book; clean off your desk; put your book away; take out your math book; and sit down." With each step, the teacher would wait until he completed one task before giving him the instruction for the next.

"What Did I Tell You to Do?"

Checking for understanding is not simply asking the child what he is supposed to do. It is a rephrasing of the direction, the use of synonyms and short, concise instructions to ensure complete understanding. "What did I tell you to do?" is an open-ended question that most of the time child is unable to answer. Continually asking such questions sounds stern and will only increase the anxiety of the child, who has done nothing wrong but is simply confused. It makes the child even more confused and unable to process the information.

Home-to-School Interventions

All the interventions described below can and should be implemented in all environments, but they should be adjusted accordingly for higher-anxiety versus lower-anxiety situations.

Breaking Tasks into Smaller Parts and Checking for Understanding

To deal with the attentional issues for children with autism spectrum disorder, we check for understanding. This is done not just by having the child repeat back what we have discussed or what we have said; we also have to use synonyms and rephrase the directions in order to see if the child is really able to generalize the skills and understand exactly what he or she is supposed to be doing. Just because children can repeat back what you said does not mean that they understand, so you will have to use many different ways of asking if they really understand.

Staying Away from Open-Ended Questions

The more open-ended questions that these children are asked, the more anxious they become. Open-ended questions also leave open the possibility for a wide range of responses. For children with Asperger's syndrome, too many choices create anxiety and fuel a feeling of being overwhelmed. It is much more effective to give a child two or three options and then let him or her choose one.

Providing Visual Cues

Visual cues are extremely important for children with Asperger's syndrome. These children have auditory processing issues, and they really benefit from having a picture to help them put the actual content of the instructions into context.

The visual cue can be a picture, the task written on the blackboard, or the task written on a chore chart at home so the children can check off exactly what they have done. This gives them a sense of completion. For children who continually have trouble with keeping their attention on a task, it also lets them know that there is an end in sight; once that task is complete, they can be motivated to focus on the next task rather than on the external stimuli that surround them.

Many children need to have each activity broken into several parts, with either verbal or tangible rewards given after each part (partial participation). If we wait until the task is complete, the child might not only lack the motivation to continue but also be unsure whether what has been completed meets the requirements or expectations.

Visual cues can also be in the form of a book in which a child chooses the activity *and* the reward that will be granted after the activity is completed. These can be attached on the same page with a space to indicate partial completion or partial participation so the child knows he or she is on the right track.

9

Communication: The Door to Friendships, Independence, and Knowledge

The issue of attention, rather than the underlying cause of abnormal language comprehension and development, has been the primary focus in the abnormal social development of Asperger's syndrome. The new focus, however, is on language difficulty as a core cognitive deficit.

Medical Perspective

Imaging studies of the brain's temporal lobe, amygdala, and hippocampus have shown deficits in people with Asperger's syndrome. Biological research raises the possibility that theory of mind is related to impairments in the parts of the brain related to communication. Deficits in language skills—including expressive (verbal), receptive (comprehension), and reciprocal skills—are a characteristic feature of individuals with Asperger's syndrome.

A lack of joint attention, or the ability to engage others by using words or gestures to share a message, has been the focus of the impairments in children with Asperger's syndrome. These children have an extremely difficult time achieving shared references in the present. They therefore might not be motivated to learn to communicate. This lack of motivation to develop language skills is one of the biggest contributors in our understanding of Asperger's syndrome. It is now known that joint attention and reciprocity in play skills are strongly correlated with language skills in autistic children, but this does not completely account for the language impairments.

For example, language acquisition may not be significantly delayed in a child with Asperger's syndrome, but affected individuals do show impairment in joint attention skills. Conversely, language-delay difficulty may be found in the parents of an autistic child or the brothers and sisters of an autistic child, even when the autistic child has good superficial language skills.

Medical Intervention

The use of SSRIs, especially Prozac, is now gaining support as a way to facilitate language and communication. There is validated research that the use of SSRIs can facilitate the speed of acquiring language skills, speech, and vocabulary enhancement. This positive effect is independent of the medication's role in reducing anxiety and enhancing mood.

Home-to-School Perspective

One of the biggest challenges for children with Asperger's syndrome is communicating with others. Zachary's biggest fear is that there will be a misunderstanding but that he won't know what the misunderstanding is. Imagine what it is like to go through life knowing that with every social interaction there is the possibility of a misunderstanding, and that when there is, you don't know how to fix it.

For example, one day we were at the garden store. While I (Melinda) was speaking with the person who worked there, Zachary and his sister, Sophie, noticed a stray cat. They decided to try to pet the cat, so they called out to it. It was quite apparent that the cat was not used to coming close to people. However, their continual persistence paid off; the cat slowly came to them and eventually allowed them to pet it.

All of a sudden, the person with whom I was speaking looked over at them and said, "You're petting the cat!" My daughter immediately knew that the person was trying to say that the cat never lets anybody touch it and how lucky they were to have that experience. My son, because he misunderstood, immediately thought he was in trouble, backed away, looked as if he was going to burst into tears, and never touched the cat again after that.

Social Blunders and Misunderstandings

There were many times that Zachary misunderstood certain situations that most people would have understood. One particular situation made me realize that I had a decision to make. When Zachary was hospitalized as an inpatient twice, at the end of fourth grade and at the beginning of fifth grade, there was a particular psychiatric technician who I immediately knew was not going to be a good match—he would cause significant misunderstandings, which would only exacerbate the problem for which Zachary had been hospitalized.

I went to visit Zachary at one of the visiting times, and he relayed a story about a misunderstanding with this psychiatric aide. The psychiatric technician asked Zachary to open the door to the cafeteria for him because he was holding a tray of food. The door was so heavy that Zachary had to use part of his body to hold the door open. The technician then said to him, "I did not tell you that you could go in there." Even though Zachary immediately knew that there had been a misunderstanding, he did not respond, nor did he self-advocate. He went directly to his room and engaged in self-injurious behavior because he felt so humiliated at what he perceived to be a great infliction from society as a whole.

My first impulse as a parent would be to go to the technician and explain that there had been a misunderstanding. What I decided to do was talk to Zachary about the decisions that he had to make.

Clarifying or Ignoring

I could continue to interpret the world for Zachary, but I knew that I would not be with him all the time, so I opted to teach him two alternatives. If he realized that there had been a misunderstanding and knew what had been misunderstood, he could clarify it; if he realized that there had been a misunderstanding but was unable to process what had been misunderstood or articulate it verbally, he could learn to be able to cope with the uncomfortable feeling of letting it go.

As a parent or an educator, you cannot clarify the world for these children in every situation, every single minute of the day. Even if you could, you would be doing them a great disservice. Part of growing up, developing socially appropriate behaviors, and learning how to generalize these skills is to have an understanding of how to clarify or have the coping mechanisms to choose not to.

When do I clarify and when do I not? It depends. I am a firm believer in providing interpretations for children, because that is how they learn. I will clarify situations for Zachary if I think they are going to have a lasting effect. I ignore situations if I think he has developed enough skill to come up with a coping mechanism in order to solve the problem on his own.

Interpreting or Enabling?

I can interpret Zachary's entire world for him and make sure that he never misunderstands anything. That would make him very happy and reduce much of his anxiety, but it would not help him to cope with situations on a continuing basis, so there is a fine line between being an interpreter and an enabler. I am not an advocate of a sink-and-swim approach. I think it is most effective to provide a safe and nurturing environment for our kids, then continually expand the boundaries to allow new opportunities and encourage risk-taking behaviors.

Nonverbal Cues

Nonverbal cues are an enormous challenge for children with Asperger's syndrome. Many of our interactions require the person who is receiving the message to interpret nonverbal cues. Most of us learn these naturally and take them for granted. Children with Asperger's syndrome need to be taught nonverbal cues, such as what a smile means and in what context, in the same way that a child has to be taught a new math concept or how to play the piano.

The Yale Child Study Center has done studies using functional MRIs to track eye movement in both the neurotypical population and people with Asperger's syndrome. The studies found that when the neurotypical population was watching a movie, the majority showed a great deal of emotion and focused on the eyes of the actors. The children with Asperger's syndrome focused on either the mouths of the actors or on some small detail on the wall of the room, such as a light switch.

Thus, we now have actual data to support what we knew empirically all along: that the nonverbal cues that most of us take for granted in interpreting messages may be interpreted completely differently by a child with Asperger's syndrome. We have to *teach* our children to learn those cues.

Conversational Skills

I would love to be able to say that I picked my children up from school and that while they interacted, I relaxed from my hard day at work. That's the way it's supposed to be, right? Not for me in this lifetime—I have to monitor every single interaction during the car ride home, during playdates, during mealtime, and again at playtime.

My objective is to see if Zachary is looking at his sister, allowing her to talk, and staying on the same topic. I monitor to see if he uses the rules of conversation, such as taking turns—pausing, then waiting for the other person to pause before speaking again—and using phrases such as "by the way" or "that reminds me" if he wants to change the subject.

At one point, I said to Zachary, "If I talk about a dog and you talk about a dog, is that a conversation?" and he replied, "Yes, Mommy." I then said, "If I talk about a dog and you talk about the beach, is that a conversation?" and he again replied, "Yes, Mommy." I realized that his definition of a conversation was simply two people standing or sitting next to each other and talking.

He did not understand the rules of conversation, such as staying on the same topic, looking at each other, taking reciprocal turns in order to keep the conversation going, asking follow-up questions, and utilizing nonverbal cues to determine whether the other person wants to keep talking.

I had to teach Zachary that when you see a child roll his eyes, it could mean that he is bored, that you are repeating yourself, that he thinks what you're saying is ridiculous, or that he wants the conversation to end. If a child just turns around and starts talking to somebody else, that might mean something different.

Zachary had to learn how to read these cues in order to be socially appropriate. Children will listen to another child go on and on about trains for only a limited amount of time. They may pay attention for a few moments, but without a lapse in the conversation or an opportunity for them to participate in the conversation as well, they will eventually leave, and that is not what we want to happen for our children. We want them to be able to maintain a conversation, give other children their turn, and acknowledge when a conversation is over.

Therefore, constant, consistent intervention during all possible social and verbal interactions is required. This is extremely tiring for a parent and nearly impossible for a classroom teacher. For every interaction that is monitored, many more slide by, and the inappropriate interactions that have not been caught and retaught will have to be changed by behavior modification.

Utilize your speech and language pathologist for these interventions. Require some of the services to be in the classroom with the other children. Require the pathologist to let you as a parent know what he or she is working on and any scripts that have been given to your child. Then make sure that every other person who is working with that child implements the exact same strategies, scripts, and cues. These services are only as good as the person implementing them and the ability of the team to generalize them in a variety of environments. Otherwise, they just stay between the child and the adult, never to leave the room.

Open-Ended Phrases

When you say to a child, "Maybe," "We'll see," "I don't know," and "What do you think?", you are using very open-ended phrases, and this is not helpful to a child with Asperger's syndrome. The child is left with a vast range of possible responses, none of which really makes any sense and all of which are so overwhelming that actually ruling out those that are not possible is a feat in itself.

The child is also left without the knowledge of what is expected of him or her, which only creates more anxiety. Until our children have developed flexibility in thinking, we should stay away from open-ended questions. They do not serve any beneficial purpose.

The same goes for open-ended responses. When children ask the same question many times a day, we cannot simply say, "I'll tell you later" or "I don't know." We have to answer their questions. If we don't, we will only perpetuate their obsession to keep asking the question until a response is given. Many of our children perseverate on a particular topic, and if it happens to be about something they do not know the answer to, they should have their questions answered. Please keep in mind that this intervention is hopefully not forever. In my experience, it is best to be concrete until the child is comfortable and feels safe. You can then start moving toward more independent interventions, such as requiring the child to look at the clock and wait five minutes. You can also write the answer on a piece of paper, and every time the child asks the question you can prompt them to look for it in their pocket. Hopefully the child will eventually think of the answer, but before asking someone else will look in their pocket and provide their own answer. This isn't perfect, but it does move, albeit slowly, from complete dependence on you toward independence.

Home-to-School Interventions

What strategies can we use to help children with communication issues? It is imperative that your treatment team include a speech-and-language pathologist who will include the teaching of pragmatics, or conversational language skills, in their sessions. Most of our children did have speech before the age of three; however, that does not mean that they had language. They could repeat a television commercial, but couldn't use their speech to engage in a conversation or to make friends. Many speech-and-language pathologists focus only on articulation and fluency, but they are trained to teach pragmatics. Find someone who is willing to be an active team member and will focus on pragmatics. However, this will be effective only if the skills that are taught are shared with all team members so they can be implemented on a consistent basis across a variety of environments.

Social Scripts

I want to differentiate between social scripts and the social stories that have so famously been created by author Carole Gray. The social script that I am talking about consists of one- or two-sentence phrases, taught either verbally or by using a visual cue (such as a flash card), that can help a child to send a message to somebody else, start a conversation, or make a need known.

I can teach a child to interact with someone on the playground by saying, "Hey, can I sit here?" That particular social script can be used in many different environments and can probably be used every day. Social scripts should be created when there are many opportunities to use them in many different settings. When children have particular social scripts, know what the possible responses are, and know how to respond to those responses, it gives them much more confidence to be able to attempt an interaction.

In first grade my son was playing tag with some of the other kids, and for some reason he was always *It*. One day he said to me, "Mommy, I don't want to be *It* anymore," and I said, "Well, then, you have to tell them," thinking that those were clear enough instructions. However, he did not understand what *tell* meant or who *them* was. He responded, "Mom what do I say?" He needed a social script, so I created the following: "You need to go up to the group of kids that you play tag with and say, 'I do not want to be *It* anymore.'"

Prediction

One of the ways that our family dealt with Zachary's tantrums when he was young was to predict for him. We did not realize that is what we were doing for about the first eighteen months of his life. All we knew was that there was a great deal of screaming and crying and that we needed it to stop. After many failed attempts of different strategies—such as consequences, time-outs, or simply leaving him at home, none of which were ideal or even worked—we began to predict every single event that took place on any given day.

"Today, we are going to Grandpa's," we would say to our son. "He is going to be sitting in the chair, and your cousins will be there. We will have peanut butter and jelly sandwiches for lunch, then we will go home. If you cry when we leave, then we will not go back next Sunday."

Predicting was an integral part of keeping the peace during our family life, and it will be integral in a classroom as well. For example, during a trip to the mall, Zachary said, "Mommy, I want to ride on that car." I could see that the car had already been taken by another child. So right away I said, "There is another child on that car. These are your choices: you can either choose another car or wait your turn, but if you scream, we will leave."

Predicting is a very necessary part of functioning through life, especially in the school setting. We need to predict every single transition for children with Asperger's syndrome and every single possible change in the schedule so they will know exactly what to expect. We would like them to eventually get to the point where they have flexibility in their thinking. If there is a change in the schedule, we want them to have had enough practice utilizing coping mechanisms to be able to acknowledge the change and comfortably accept it.

It is natural to think that if we interact with children with Asperger's syndrome in the way that the rest of the world would interact with them—such as by not adapting the world around them but by allowing the unexpected to happen on a daily basis—that this will eventually desensitize the children to the unexpected. We like to think that if we do this long enough, these children will eventually come around and realize that everything is okay and that the world is not going to fall apart.

I have not found this to be the case, however. In fact, what I have found is the exact opposite. If children with Asperger's syndrome are forced by well-meaning teachers, therapists, and parents to "just deal with it" because that's what life is really like, they will never build the confidence to attempt any flexibility in their thinking, take risks, or adjust to the unexpected. They have never had the foundation that is required to build the trust to gain those skills. Those who have been given a strong foundation over many years will eventually trust the flexibility of the world.

When my son was in first grade, I told him I would pick him up at 2:30 p.m. every day at a particular bench, and I made sure I did so without fail. We did this for about five months, until he realized that he could count on me to be true to my word.

Then I changed one variable. "I am going to pick you up at two thirty, but I am going to pick you up at either the front gate or the bench, so you will have to look for me in those two places." After about three months, I changed a second variable. "I'll pick you up at either the bench or the front gate, and sometime between two thirty and two forty-five." This timeline worked for Zachary, but you have to determine what timeline is best for your child. You will know you can move on when your child feels comfortable and anxiety is at a minimum.

This entire process took approximately a year, and after many years of practice Zachary was able to wait for me and look for me, and if for some reason I didn't show up at the expected time or place, he knew to go into the school office and call me.

Emotional Conversations

Emotional conversations are very difficult for children with Asperger's syndrome, because emotions are very ambiguous and can change at a moment's notice without any warning. Changes in emotion are accompanied by different facial expressions and nonverbal cues. Because emotions are so unpredictable, Zachary had to be taught how to have an emotional conversation, just as one must learn to play the piano.

At night, when we put him to bed and we encouraged him to talk, the rules were as follows: "You have to talk about something that has to do with a person or a feeling; you cannot talk about a thing, and you cannot talk about your current interest." We kept him on track for about ten to fifteen minutes every night. At one point he said, "Mommy, these conversations make me very uncomfortable," and I replied, "I know, and that is why we have to do it."

As he has grown up, he has become more and more comfortable with feelings and emotional conversations and will even initiate an emotional conversation. Sometimes he wants to tell me something related to an emotion, and he will tell me that he wants to tell me, but then he will say, "No, never mind, never mind." It takes me fifteen to twenty minutes to get it out of him, but that is a great improvement from when he was not able to have any emotional conversations at all.

Consistent Monitoring

There has to be consistent monitoring of playdates with friends and interactions with siblings, because the only way to ensure that appropriate communication is happening is to watch to see if it happens and, when necessary, prompt the children to use the conversational rules. Otherwise, many conversational interactions pass by that are not appropriate, that don't follow the rules, and then those errors are embedded in children with Asperger's syndrome as the correct way to interact with somebody. Once that happens, these habits are very difficult to change.

Strategies Based on the Child's Perception

In many ways, children with Asperger's syndrome have a one-sided perception of the world. For example, if you and I build a house out of LEGO bricks, my side might have the front door and your side might have two windows. We would each be able to acknowledge that even though we can't see the other side, it is different than our own. A child with Asperger's might often think that if they have built a side of a LEGO house with two windows, then every side looks exactly like theirs. They are not able to recognize or comprehend that the other sides can be different. Therefore, if you were to ask them whether their LEGO house has a door, it would not be uncommon for them to say no.

What do we do about this? Ideally, we would like for them to be able to see that each person may have a different perception of the same situation. Some of our children will indeed develop that way. For others, however, it may take a long time to happen or might never happen. Nevertheless, we are still responsible for teaching them the rules.

At the end of fourth grade and the beginning of fifth grade, Zachary was hospitalized at the Neuropsychiatric Institute at UCLA for self-injurious behaviors. His perception was that when he had engaged in some bad behavior, it required a physical punishment. I would tell him, "Daddy and I don't believe in spanking" and "Everything is okay. Saying I'm sorry is enough." His response was that saying "I'm sorry" did not make him feel as if justice had been served and thus did not make him feel any better. He therefore decided that he was going to implement the physical punishment himself.

I continued to think that if I talked to Zachary long enough, he would eventually understand my point of view. After an hour, I realized that what I had to work with was a child who thought that any inappropriate action required a physical punishment. I had no choice. I had to say, "Fine, if you are so sure that this action deserves a punishment, then come to me, and I will give you the punishment." Then, at least, I had control of what the punishment was and could make sure that it was not physical. Even when I thought that no punishment at all was necessary, I had to provide an intervention that would satisfy my son's perception of the situation, not my own.

I am working with a child in whom I have yet to see any indication that he is able to understand that others can have a different perception of the same situation. For example, once he left his classroom very upset and ran across the playground to another area. When I finally found him, I said, "I do not want you to ever do that again. It's not safe; we were scared and did not know where you were." His response was, "I was right here."

I said, "How would I know that? My office is on the other end of the campus. I do not supervise any of the teachers who have classes over here, and there is no way that I would know that you were sitting over here." His response again was, "I was right here," and then he concluded by saying, "And if three people cannot find me, then maybe they are not fit to work here."

No amount of speaking to this child or trying to show him that there was another perspective did any good. In such a case, when teaching another perspective is not a possibility, the priority becomes the objective of the lesson, which in this case was safety. Therefore, regardless of the boy's inability to see others' perceptions, he had to be taught the rule that "You may not leave without permission." We must provide strategies through the child's perception rather than our own, or no learning can take place.

Zachary has seen several different psychologists, all of whom assured me that they had worked with children with Asperger's syndrome, but several of whom did not understood anything about these children. Once, Zachary entered a project in an art contest. He was one of only two students chosen to participate, which was a great accomplishment. It turned out that the other child won in the division and Zachary did not. Needless to say, he was quite upset.

Our weekly therapy session happened to be that day. Perfect. The psychologist would get him to understand, I thought. So we went into the psychologist's office, and the psychologist proceeded to tell him that winning meant many different things to many different people: trying your best, simply participating, and being chosen at all.

What he failed to realize was that Zachary's perception was that you enter a contest and someone judges and picks a winner. If the judge doesn't pick you, you haven't won. Period. The clinician should have provided Zachary with therapy that worked within his own definition of winning, because at that point Zachary was unable to see anyone else's point of view.

Unfortunately, the therapist did not understand this, and the learning opportunity was lost. Zachary's response upon leaving that session was, "Mom, I didn't believe one thing that guy said." My response to him was, "I know. We won't go back."

Upon Zachary's discharge from his last hospitalization, I was required by the treatment team to identify the psychologist who would be treating him as soon as he was released. I did as I was asked, but I was skeptical that it would be beneficial. Again I found someone who assured me that he understood the complexities of a child with Asperger's syndrome and could definitely treat a child just discharged from the inpatient unit.

Zachary had been admitted due to severe depression and anxiety that resulted in self-injurious behaviors. Even upon arriving home, the self-injurious behaviors had not completely ceased, and Zachary was attending school with bruises on his forehead, where he had hit himself with his fists, a baseball bat, or other objects. I called ahead to the psychologist to let him know that this had been a bad week and what to expect. We arrived, Zach went into his session, and I spent the fifty-minute session drinking tea.

When Zach's session ended, I took one look at his face and knew we were in trouble. The psychologist had no idea. Zachary was in complete hysterics and was hitting me the whole time I drove home. When I arrived home I immediately called the psychologist and explained what happened. I asked him to share with me what had happened in the session. He was absolutely shocked at what I had to tell him, but after hearing about the session, I was not surprised. Zachary had walked in, and the conversation went something like this:

Psychologist: How are you?

Zachary: Fine.

Psychologist: What is that on your head?

Zachary: A bruise.

Psychologist: How did you get that bruise?

Zachary: I hit myself.

Psychologist: I thought you said you were fine.

Zachary: I am fine.

Psychologist: Zachary, if you don't tell me the truth, this is not going to work.

Those who are familiar with the characteristics of Asperger's syndrome know that these children rarely, if ever, lie about anything, and even when it appears as though they are lying, it is usually due to a misperception of a situation. In addition, these children are very literal. When the psychologist asked Zachary how he was and Zachary said he was fine, that was the truth, because at that moment he *was* fine.

The moral of the story: Therapy can help, but pick and choose a therapist very carefully, because misunderstandings such as those above not only are counterproductive, because they do not provide strategies or learning within the child's perspective, they can also have long-lasting repercussions on the child's ability to build trust with others.

10

Anxiety and Depression: Worries and Sadness

Anxiety and depression are common in Asperger's syndrome.

Medical Perspective

The special challenge from a pharmacological point of view is the high relapse rate after the cessation of medication. I (Syed) usually treat children with SSRIs such as Prozac for nine to eighteen months, then I take them off for twelve to eighteen months. Approximately 50 percent of children relapse within the first year. Approximately 60 percent of the children in my practice have to go back on the drug.

Brain maturation affects the percentage of children who are able to be weaned off medication. In the general population, the ratio of anxiety and depression is about equal in prepubescent girls and boys. After the onset of puberty, the rate is twice as high in boys. Weaning a girl off medication for anxiety and depression after the onset of puberty is much more difficult than weaning a boy off the medication due to sensitive hormonal differences.

Successful weaning off of medication is directly related to what is called the *slow taper protocol*. For example, I would reduce the dosage by a quarter every week or two. The child's system needs time to adjust and start replacing what is missing. The receptors will take a longer time to start working on their own. I have found that I achieve better results with this slow and methodical approach.

Medical Intervention

Long-term data on SSRI usage in the treatment of obsessive-compulsive disorders has led to a growing interest in its usage in Asperger's syndrome as well. There is significant evidence of abnormalities in serotonin function in children with Asperger's syndrome. This is also the case in depressive mood disorders. This has led to its increasing usage in this disorder. Whereas the clinical evidence is robust for the treatment of anxiety, treatment for depression with SSRI has produced mixed results.

SSRIs are potentially useful for the treatment of repetitive behaviors, anxiety, irritability, self-injurious behavior, depression, and aggression in Asperger's syndrome. However, the safety of these drugs has recently been questioned by society, physicians, and the FDA, so close monitoring is required.

Although research supports the benefits of SSRIs in children, there is less evidence of their effectiveness in adults with Asperger's syndrome. The side effects include aggression, an increase in self-injurious behavior, suicidality, anxiety, agitation, hostility, hypomania, and significant euphoric mood. The practice is to start children at an extremely low dosage and slowly accelerate the concentration. The expected response rate is approximately

40 to 50 percent in children with Asperger's syndrome and comorbid mood disorders.

Home-to-School Perspective

Children with Asperger's syndrome seem to run a great risk of anxiety and depression because they are starting to become aware that their interests are different, the way they process the world is different, and they are not part of the interactions that are taking place among their peers. I (Melinda) have found in my professional life that the more of an impact this disorder has on a child, the less of a chance he or she has to deal with anxiety and/or depression. This is because a child who is more afflicted with this syndrome is less likely to have an awareness of the world around them, thus having less of a risk of anxiety or depression. Children who are mildly affected have more of an awareness of the world around them, resulting in anxiety or depression because they see what they are missing, they know what is difficult for them and that they are not able to change or fix it, and they are aware that others don't think or feel the same way they do.

What Do Our Children Worry About?

Children with Asperger's syndrome worry about anything, from real-life issues such as a parent dying or having car accident to topics that appear to be completely irrational, such as when my son questioned whether I was really me. I came home after seeing the movie *A Beautiful Mind*, and Zachary had been watching a cartoon that night in which the characters visited a town only to find that it wasn't the way they had left it.

Needless to say, Zachary was quite upset. I asked him why this upset him so, and he replied, "Mommy, how do I know that you are you? I know that I am me, because I am me, but how do I know that you are you?"

How do you comfort a child who is anxious about something so abstract and existential? I took his hand, placed it on my face, and said, "This is how you know. You are touching me, not you." I know that this didn't really explain to Zachary that I really was who I said I was, but touching my face made me real to him, and therefore he trusted me.

What Causes the Depression?

Depression is another matter. It is not only terrifying for parents but also extremely frightening for the children. They do not understand why they feel so sad all the time, and sometimes they are quite unable to articulate how they are feeling. Caretakers need to be on the lookout for a change in personality, a change in sleep patterns, an inability to enjoy what this particular child normally enjoys, and a continual sadness that is not explained by a particular situation. True clinical depression should be treated by a professional who specializes in that issue. If you are unsure whether the child's depression is situational or clinical, err on the side of caution.

For children who are sad due to a particular situation, such as lack of friends, different interests, and just plain feeling that they don't fit in, we look for ways to make them feel successful about themselves by using their own interests. If they are obsessed with trains, we try to encourage them to talk about trains, do a report on trains, or express their skill and their strength to the rest of the class so that the class realizes that this child has something unique and interesting to offer.

Sameness, Predictability, and Closure to Activities

Children with Asperger's syndrome have a need for sameness and predictability in their routine. Our children really struggle with unexpected change and transition time, because they don't have a sense of closure or a sense of what is going to happen next.

There are definitely behavioral strategies that will help. I am not necessarily advocating for or against medication; it is simply another viable option. However, my personal experience is that my son would not be able to function without medication for anxiety and depression. He truly needs to have the medication to be able to cope with everyday life.

If you have a child who is incredibly anxious, and it is affecting his or her behavior, that is absolutely not the time to ask the child to use coping skills to control the anxiety. Medication allows children time to think about the choices they have and either make a conscious decision or ask someone else to help them.

Many parents are very leery of medications or absolutely against medications, and they should be cautious. My advice is to do your own research: review the clinical studies, get a second opinion, and contact the physicians who conducted the studies to find out everything you can about that medication. If the medication is changing your child's personality or causing so many side effects that the benefit is not outweighing the disadvantages, then either the medication is not right or the dosage is not right.

When medication works, it reduces that child's baseline anxiety or depression and allows the treatment team a little bit more access. It allows the child to be able to take in the strategies that the caretaker, the therapist, or the teacher is trying to teach and to understand what has been discussed and then possibly apply it in another situation. If the baseline anxiety and depression are so high that there is no time to intervene with strategies, then you are fighting an uphill battle.

Home-to-School Interventions

Children with Asperger's syndrome are comforted by sameness in routines and schedules. Not only do we capitalize on this as a classroom strategy, but best practices teach us to put schedules on the board and even a particular schedule on a child's desk. Sometimes we laminate the schedules and have the children check off the activities they complete as they finish them because it gives them a sense of closure and they will know what to expect the next time.

If there is a change in the routine, we are able to change it on the schedules. Some children require picture schedules; some just need word schedules; then, as a classroom strategy each morning, the teacher reviews the schedule for the day and any changes that might take place. This way the child will always know what to expect. Parents can use this same strategy at home for chores, family activities, special events, and daily routines such as getting dressed, putting on shoes, brushing teeth, and eating breakfast.

Prediction

Once again, prediction is a lifesaver. Predictions will reduce anxiety in a way that nothing else will. Long before Zachary was diagnosed, we were predicting: who was going to be at the birthday party, what we were going to have for dinner, how many people were going to be at Grandma's, and what would happen if one of his cousins did not respond in a way that he expected. All I knew was that letting him know ahead of time what was going to come up reduced tension and seemed to alleviate his fears.

It wasn't until our daughter was born and started to talk that I realized we did not interact with her in the same way that we interacted with Zachary. We would not have survived as a family if we had not implemented predictions in every single situation all day long. Due to the consistency of this strategy, Zachary now has a solid foundation for knowing what he can count on. As he has grown older, he has been more willing to take risks and has become much more flexible.

Now that he is seventeen, we very rarely have to predict any-thing. However, even at this older age, there are still times when predicting is appropriate, such as how to ask a manager at a bookstore if they have any job openings. Sometimes I might suddenly realize that we have to go to the market, and he might say, "Mom, you know I don't like it when you don't tell me things ahead of time," whereas five years ago, that change in routine without a prediction would have caused such a fit of rage that he would have been hiding under the bed for three hours, hiding in the closet, throwing things, or doing a variety of other inappropriate behaviors.

Knowledge of Expectations

Without a doubt, the knowledge of expectations reduces anxiety and depression simply because the children know ahead of time what is going to happen next. We all like to know what is going to happen, which is why we like to hear a weather report, watch the previews of next week's TV show, or look at the program before a musical begins. It is human nature to want to know what is coming next. However, neurotypical people can cope without such knowledge without much discomfort. For children with Asperger's syndrome, it is almost painful, psychologically, and it causes an inability to learn skills that would help the children in the future.

Transition Objects

One of the ways we can help children, especially young children, reduce anxiety is to give them transition objects that are affiliated with the next activity. In a classroom, for example, if you are reading and then it is time for recess, children who are not done with their reading activity do not want to transition to the new activity until they are completely done. Thus, if the next activity is recess, you could hand the children a ball, which would be the transition object.

The transition object must always be related to the upcoming activity, or the children will not be able to make the connection. For example, if children at recess have been given a five-minute warning to line up (which is followed by a three-minute and then a one-minute warning), and they still do not want to line up, a proactive approach would be to hand them an item related to the next activity while they are still outside. If the next activity is math, hand the children math manipulatives or a calculator.

The same technique can be used at home. Transition objects, such as books, blankets, or toys that have been specifically designated for transition time, will motivate a child to move to the next activity. However, parents need to make sure that these items are used *only* for transition time; otherwise the importance of the item and its association is lost.

Partial Participation

Partial participation is of utmost importance because most children with Asperger's syndrome cannot finish an entire activity in one sitting. We want to make sure that we give them feedback and acknowledgment for partial participation. We might have to break up an assignment into five or ten parts, and what would normally take a half an hour could take three days at ten minutes each day. It is a very appropriate classroom strategy to give a child one section of an assignment at a time, with a preferred activity in between to keep him or her motivated.

Many children require accommodations and modifications for classroom work. Accommodations are supports that allow the child to access the grade-level content but that don't change the content, such as one-to-one instruction, small-group instruction, preferential seating, extended time, and the rephrasing of directions. Modifications actually change the content of the assignment, such as allowing an eighth grader to work on multiplication. It is still a math assignment during math time, but the achievement standard has been lowered to meet the child's needs.

Appropriate Timing of Interventions

We need to look at what exacerbates the child's anxiety and what relieves it. The timing of an intervention is extremely important in this regard. I observed a young girl who was included in regular education but who had been diagnosed with fragile X syndrome and had many autistic manifestations of that genetic disorder. I realized that she would easily have a meltdown in about six minutes. She could probably sit in her chair for four to five minutes, but after that her anxiety would get the best of her and that would be it; we would not have any access to her.

The objective was to provide her with an opportunity for a break, another choice, or another peer with whom to interact before the six minutes was up so that she would have consecutive successes with her behavior and be positively reinforced for those successes. At four to five minutes, when she was still able to actually make a choice, we asked her if she needed a break or would like to do something else. That way, we were allowing her to self-advocate and remain in control of herself. If we handled this right, we would catch her before she began escalating, and then those particular choices would become rewards for appropriate behavior. It is all a matter of timing.

Many of us respond to anxiety in different ways; some are calm and rational, whereas others, like me, are not. When I was typing my dissertation and the computer crashed, I did not want to be taught how to fix it or listen to my husband go through a task analysis, I just wanted him to fix it. I had a hard time being patient and controlling my frustration.

Thus, with children with Asperger's syndrome, who already have trouble with this, why would we expect them to be able use every coping skill they have at the height of their anxiety?

It is the job of the treatment team to provide an intervention at the appropriate time. For some children, the more words that are used when they are anxious, the more anxious they become. The teacher, parent, therapist, or other adult should take a few moments to sit and listen rather than talk.

The basic guiding rule is that the louder the children become, either at home or at school, the quieter you should become—and perhaps stop talking altogether. The last thing an anxious child wants to see is parents or teachers responding to their own anxiety rather than the child's situation. Children look to adults to provide boundaries and keep them safe. If we are out of control, we will not be able to help them gain control.

Children with Asperger's syndrome have enough difficulty processing language in calm circumstances, much less when they are anxious. I cannot emphasize too strongly that this is *not* the time to try to have a heart-to-heart talk. Keep your sentences concise so that there is no extraneous verbiage for the children to have to process.

11

Sensory Needs or Avoidance: Itchy Clothes, Smelly Food, Noisy Rooms

Severe sensory issues, such as oversensitivity to smells, textures of clothes, and a variety of sounds (loud sounds, regular sounds, and the noise of a crowd), are frequent in Asperger's syndrome. Sensory needs can also sometimes manifest as getting too close to another individual or touching inappropriately because of a need for tactile stimulation.

Medical Perspective

Sensitivity to sensory stimuli is a red flag for Asperger's syndrome. However, it can sometimes be misinterpreted as only a problem with sensory integration. This will lead the parents to seek occupational therapy interventions without thoroughly addressing the bigger picture, the social problems in Asperger's syndrome.

I (Syed) have seen children diagnosed with pragmatic-semantic language disorders or a nonverbal learning disability without the socialization of the child being taken into consideration for the diagnosis, thereby resulting in the child being diagnosed with the symptoms of Asperger's syndrome rather than the condition itself. Such symptomatology should immediately raise the suspicion of Asperger's syndrome.

Sometimes the high cognitive level of these individuals—they often have extraordinary intelligence and memory, often remembering even trivial events from the remote past—leads families and practitioners to the correct diagnosis. This symptomatology generally manifests with a verbal IQ that is much higher than performance IQ, and it can mask some of the core symptoms of the disorder.

Medical Intervention

In the rare cases in which sensory integration therapy has not worked, I have used medications with mild to moderate success. I try to avoid using antipsychotic medications for these symptoms because the long-term risk-benefit ratio is not very clear to me.

It is imperative that occupational therapists take a lead role in addressing the issues related to hypersensitivity to smell, sound, sight, touch, and taste issues. Medication is not an answer to food issues, in particular, such as needing meals to be pureed. Some antipsychotic medications do help with these sensitivity issues, but for the most part, the issues have to be addressed with behavioral intervention.

Home-to-School Perspective

Let me (Melinda) describe a scenario to you. You are listening to a lecture that lasts for an hour, but instead of sitting in a chair, you are sitting on the floor with your legs straight out in front of you. Most, if not all, of you could probably do this, barring any sort of physical or medical issue. However, at some point during the hour, you might have to readjust yourself to get the kind of sensory input that you need to continue concentrating on what the lecturer is saying, because otherwise the position would start to make you uncomfortable.

Now let me give you a couple of examples of children with Asperger's syndrome.

Joey does not like to sit on his bottom. He either sits on his heels with the heels on the seat of the chair or stands by his desk with one knee on the chair, the other foot on the floor, and the rest of his body leaning across his desk. He puts his elbows on the table, puts his face in his hands, or is constantly holding something or playing with something that is usually not needed for the assignment. This is the child who is flicking a pencil, chewing his hair, playing with paper clips, or squeezing a ball.

Emily becomes agitated before every tabletop activity. She is frustrated, she cannot attend to a task, her hands are constantly moving, and she continually gets out of her seat—not because she can't sit still, but because everything around her distracts her: the air conditioner, the talking of her peers, the sound of pencils scratching against paper. Her peripheral vision catches everything on the sly: a piece of paper floating off a desk, an eraser rolling onto the floor, dust particles descending from a ceiling vent, and the adults in the room moving among the students to provide assistance.

Joey and Emily are examples of students who are seeking sensory input or are trying to aviod it.

Sensory-Seeking and Sensory-Avoiding Behaviors

Combine all these sensory-seeking and sensory-avoiding behaviors with language-processing difficulties, social misunderstandings, and possible anxiety and depression because those around you can't hear the pencils against the paper or the air conditioning vent turning on. What you have is a child on complete overload, very possibly without the ability to articulate what exactly is too overwhelming or what exactly is needed for him or her to attend. Such children feel sheer frustration at the fact that no one understands why they are angry, why they can't pay attention, or why they need to get out of their seats or shake their hands for no apparent reason.

Hypersensitivity to Stimuli

Many children with Asperger's syndrome are hypersensitive to sensory stimuli. They cannot tolerate certain sounds, they cannot tolerate anybody touching them, or they cannot tolerate touch that is either too light or deep in pressure. There are children who can hear things that we cannot hear.

I knew a child who had trouble riding in a car because he could hear the tires creating friction on the road. My own son was fit to be tied when we couldn't find the cricket that had decided to take up residence in our home. I have met children who have to have the tags cut out of all their clothes because they feel too scratchy, or they can wear only certain kinds of socks, or the elastic in the socks has to be a certain way. There are children who will eat only a certain color or texture of food.

The same goes for smell and sight. In fact, at our school, we do not have a cafeteria for exactly this reason. Our children are so hypersensitive to smells that mixing the variety of smells the way a cafeteria does is asking for trouble.

All of these things affect the classroom environment and affect how successful children are in a classroom situation. These reactions are not merely annoying to the teacher, although they might be. More importantly, these reactions can be intrusive enough to cause significant behaviors and effect learning new skills, including the ability to concentrate and to improve upon social skills. A noisy cafeteria might be intolerable, therefore requiring the student to eat inside the classroom, missing out on a social opportunity. Sensitivity toward food colors and textures can single out a child who can't participate in the pizza party. A humming air conditioner might be so loud to children with Asperger's syndrome that it physically causes them pain; they might then have to be removed from the classroom, requiring them to miss a lesson.

Home-to-School Interventions

If you have children who are very distracted by sounds, you do not want to put them by an air conditioner vent or by an open door. Classroom teachers should pair children who are the most sensitive with others who are having the same challenges. This way instruction can be provided in small groups, in possibly another setting. Earphones that can block out extraneous sound should be available during independent work, fire drills, and transitions, if necessary. If you have children who are distracted by light, outside noise, or movement seen through a window, then covering the windows might be the way to go.

Desensitization

Sometimes it might be necessary to implement cognitive behavioral intervention to desensitize a child to a particular environment. The basic guiding rule is to determine if, in fact, the particular environment has to be used on a consistent basis. A classroom obviously fits that criterion; dinner at Aunt Mary's once a year might not.

One might create an environment that is very sparse, and then as the children become more accustomed to it, the teacher can begin the desensitization process by adding classroom-friendly items to the room—maybe one mobile, one chart, or one picture on the wall, and so on, with the intention that eventually the children will get used to being in a typical-looking classroom.

A regular kindergarten classroom can and usually does look like an absolute circus, every inch of board, wall, and even ceiling covered with projects done by the children. This might please the parents, but it can be very overwhelming to a five-year-old child, especially one on the autistic spectrum.

At a very young age, Zachary was afraid of grass. He wouldn't walk on it, touch it, or even go near it. I began by having Zach just sit on the driveway for several days, then move a bit closer each day, until finally he was sitting directly next to the grass. We then picked some blades to hold, and we did this for several days. The culmination of this process was a picnic on the grass, utilizing highly preferred activities and toys to motivate him to stay there.

We want our children to be able to be in a typical age-appropriate social environment and not be distracted, upset, or agitated by things, or at least to be able to utilize coping skills to tolerate them.

Self-Stimulatory Behaviors

Many children with Asperger's syndrome engage in self-stimulatory behaviors. The most well-known, stereotypical behavior is hand-flapping. However, that is not the only self-stimulatory behavior these children have, and some do not have this behavior at all. Children with Asperger's syndrome can have behaviors such as waving their hands in front of their faces, constantly picking at their fingers, making noises with their mouths, or feeling the need to stand up and move their legs.

These self-stimulatory behaviors serve a purpose. We all have them. Think about the last time you had lunch with a friend, sat in a conference, or spoke on the phone. Did your twirl your hair while waiting for lunch, shake your foot during the conference, or doodle on a pad while speaking on the phone? All are self-stimulatory behaviors that keep us attending to the particular task in which we are engaged. However, ours are age-appropriate, fairly discreet, and don't interfere with our accomplishment of the activity.

Meeting the Need Another Way

Our children's self-stimulatory behaviors can at times be very disruptive unless we are there to set boundaries, interpret what needs are actually being met by these behaviors, and then meet these needs in other ways. This is where creativity comes in. We cannot and should not assume that the children will be able to articulate why they like to flap their hands, spin in circles, or bang into walls.

For example, I observed a student in middle school who would constantly tap a pencil against the desk, which was very distracting to all the other students in the class. Our job was to figure out what kind of sensory input that student was receiving for that behavior. Was it the movement of his hand? Was it the fact that he could see the movement, therefore providing visual input, or was it actually the sound of the behavior? It turned out that it was actually the movement of his hand that was reinforcing to him. Therefore, we had him tap on his leg rather than on the desk. This provided him with the same sensory input that he needed, but it did not distract everybody else.

When Do You Intervene?

My basic guiding rule is that if the behavior does not inhibit learning or social development for either the child with Asperger's syndrome or the people around him or her, then we ignore it. Just because it is distracting to us is not a reason to intervene. Children do many things that annoy adults simply because they are children. If the behavior is socially appropriate, we leave it alone. If the behaviors are very noticeable and are preventing social interaction, then we need to do something about them.

It is our job to figure out what the need is and provide a more appropriate behavior that meets the same need.

The Role of the Occupational Therapist

Sensory processing is when the brain recognizes and responds on input from the various senses. Sensory integration occurs when the brain then processes the information and is able to respond appropriately to its environment. The child can perform motor planning skills, such as walking up stairs, and otherwise interact with his environment. However, when a child has sensory integration dysfunction, as many of our children with Asperger's syndrome do, then the actual deficit may present as inattentiveness, balance issues, and even aggression.

Sometimes it is very, very difficult to determine what need is being met by the behaviors or what is being avoided by the behaviors. This is where occupational therapists come in. They are the most experienced on proprioceptive input and vestibular input. *Proprioceptive* sense refers to the sensory input and feedback that tells us about movement and body positions. *Vestibular* input is determined through the receptors in your inner ear that control your balance. Occupational therapists are an important part of the treatment team in terms of figuring out how to regulate a child's system and, more ideally, how to teach the child to self-regulate. I have simplified this role a great deal but, hopefully, I have not simplified the importance.

Identifying the Need

When we have children with behavioral problems in the classroom, we have to look at whether it is strictly a behavioral issue or if the behavior is being triggered by a sensory issue. Is the child is not doing his math because the tag on his shirt is bothering him, but he does not have the word recall to let someone know?

Is the child hitting the child next to her because the other child just had tuna fish for lunch and she cannot stand the smell? Those kinds of things happen all the time, and sometimes they are not so obvious. It is our job to find out exactly why a certain behavior is taking place and then work with the treatment team to provide a more appropriate behavior for the child.

What about Opting Out?

If children cannot tolerate certain sounds, this sometimes leaves parents and educators with just one choice: to opt out of a certain activity. When I have to make this decision for my son, I always ask myself if this is a situation that he will face throughout his life. In other words, is it worth putting him through this activity because it is a skill he needs to have? Is it something he should learn to tolerate because he is going to have to do it often for a long time?

School is an activity that he will have to endure for many years to come, so he needs to learn appropriate coping strategies. In addition, the only way one realizes the benefits of having friends is to play with friends. Therefore, children with Asperger's syndrome need many playdates, although they will be difficult.

However, a school play might be something that you can opt out of. A birthday party of an acquaintance who is seen once a year is another. An adult activity, such as a dinner party, which is a novel environment, might be another. This is a personal decision that will vary from family to family as well as from classroom to classroom. Obviously, a teacher has a bit less flexibility, but it is not impossible.

Life is short, and our kids should not have to tolerate everything that comes their way. They can opt out of activities, and as they get older they will choose to do so. As adults, we opt out of activities all the time: another family get-together, dinner with annoying Uncle Fred, or a dreaded workout.

The Dreaded Mealtime

Food issues are common in children with Asperger's syndrome. I have never worked with any child who died of starvation from eating only three different foods. Food issues can include refusal to eat something that is a certain color, a lack of tolerance for certain textures, and a refusal to eat certain food groups. Certainly we want to make sure that our children get all the vitamins and minerals they need, but there are other ways to do that. The bigger issue you make of a meal, the longer it will last and the more difficult it will become to change. The last thing you want is for food to be an issue at every single meal. Just as desensitization needs to happen for fears, it also needs to happen for food textures, groups and colors. Change needs to be made in small increments, changing only one variable at a time. In other words, success will be limited if you change the color, the texture, and the food item all at once. You might have to start with a food item that is a color the child doesn't like but that smells very appetizing. If you pair this with his or her favorite person sitting there or reading a favorite story, you might have some luck. Keep track of the combinations you have tried and eliminate those that don't work. There are sneaky ways to get in vegetables and fruit, such as in smoothies or muffins.

Sensory Accommodations

In the classroom, we watch the children who sit on their heels, who lean across their desks, who have their elbows on the table, or who stand on one leg with the other knee resting on the chair. Teachers constantly react to these alternative ways of sitting by saying, "Sit down," "Sit up straight," "Put your head up," "Sit still," and other such instructions.

It seems natural to some adults to say such things to children, partly because we think that children can better attend to a lesson if they sit the way we want them to, but sometimes it is because it is just plain annoying to us. Parents and teachers must resist the urge to constantly "correct" children who are simply sitting in ways that are more comfortable for them.

Many children with Asperger's syndrome constantly need to be moving, which is a more difficult issue than different ways of sitting. There must be limits, especially in the classroom, and that's where structured sensory breaks are very effective. For example, a child might do some jumping jacks or play with a jump rope directly before engaging in a table-top activity. The occupational therapist might implement a strategy to have the child press the palms of his hands on the seat of the chair while sitting in order to provide that input before such an activity. Seated activities may be limited to a short amount of time with sensory breaks in between. These breaks may include hugging a ball, playing with play dough, curling up in a bean bag, or simply walking around the room. Once the break is complete, the child will sit back down for another session. The use of a timer is very effective, as it gives the child an ending to the activity or the break. This way, the sensory need is met but in a controlled, limited way.

In my son's case, he needed to sit with his heels or knees on the seat of the chair In fact, when he was directed to sit on his bottom, he was unable to focus and complete a tabletop task. Therefore, I made sure that everybody involved in his education knew that he simply needed to sit a certain way, so they did not redirect him to sit on his bottom. Many teachers ask me, "How do you know that he is not taking advantage and just wants to get up or move around?" or "Maybe all the other children will want to do this as well." If a child is sitting this way or is leaning across the table, as long as he or she is not distracting the person next to him or her and there is no safety issue involved, then it is fine to let the child sit in the way that is most comfortable. Leave well enough alone and choose your battles carefully.

Children who have sensory issues and are redirected to "sit on your bottom" or "sit still" may be able to do so for a short period, but they will eventually be right back on their heels or knees or leaning across their desks. Children who don't have such sensory issues are more likely to stay in the redirected position for a longer amount of time.

Children with sensory issues can be helped with self-regulating activities, such as hanging on monkey bars before coming to class, using clay or other substances to squeeze before beginning to work, or using items such as LEGOs to gain focus through fine motor and detailed physical activity.

I cannot stress enough the importance of occupational therapists. They are able to provide therapeutic interventions and proactive strategies to help children access the academic curriculum and participate in social interaction in a more meaningful and consistent way.

12

Behavior as Communication: I Will Make You Understand Even If My Words Don't Make Sense

Children with Asperger's syndrome have poor frustration tolerance and a high level of irritability. These symptoms, as part of Asperger's syndrome, are often misdiagnosed as primary mood disorder or primary anxiety disorder. When frustration and irritability are combined with impulsiveness, an adolescent may be diagnosed with conduct disorder or oppositional defiance disorder. Such misdiagnoses have produced disastrous results in schools and in residential homes.

Medical Perspective

Children with Asperger's syndrome tend to be very impression-able, so they can sometimes acquire the behaviors of both con-duct disorder and oppositional defiance disorder. Please note that children with Asperger's syndrome can pick up or absorb traits from adults and other children with significant behavior and conduct issues, including boundary issues, getting too close to people, inappropriate touching or hugging, and overall poor social relatedness.

Poor and inappropriate social relatedness is a challenge to diagnose. It consists of an overall deficit in appreciating the needs and the perspectives of others, a lack of theory of mind (empathy). It is often incorrectly evaluated by clinicians, result-ing in a misdiagnosis and the poor overall management of the individuals.

The characteristics of poor social relatedness are noticeable at an early age. These children grab their toys, will not share them with others, and, as they become older, insist that their demands be met immediately. These children become frustrated easily, often resulting in explosive behavior. These are some of the clues to appropriately diagnosing Asperger's syndrome versus a pure primary mood disorder. It is my (Syed's) observation that adolescent boys are particularly demanding and abusive toward their mothers.

On many occasions, the lack of a correct diagnosis of Asperger's syndrome has resulted in treatment that is geared toward a mixed affective disorder. Inappropriate medication has then been used, with very poor results. The frequent mistaking of aggression in Asperger's syndrome for bipolar disorder is one of the more com-mon challenges in clinical practice.

Medical Intervention

The treatment of complex disorders like Asperger's syndrome brings a particular challenge to pharmacotherapy. Setting realistic expectations about the benefits of medication is necessary. The target symptoms are very difficult to manage, and it is important for the clinician to emphasize that these medications are not a panacea for the treatment of many difficult cases. Medications work in conjunction with behavior modification, educational structure, and a variety of other therapies, which form the model to bring about improvement in individuals with this difficult disorder.

Antipsychotic Medications

The antipsychotic medications Risperdal (risperidone) and aripirazole (Abilify) are used to treat severe irritability, aggression, and self-injurious behavior in autistic children ages five to seventeen. Physical aggression and self-harm can be a significant issue in adolescents especially, because of their larger size and physical strength. This creates an atmosphere of danger not only toward themselves but also toward others.

In the absence of successful behavioral interventional therapy, antipsychotic medications have been found to be very effective with these individuals and are widely used. These medications are not the intervention of choice, but only an intervention of second choice—after nonmedicinal interventions have failed in the management of behavior.

The potential negative side effects of antipsychotics include tardive dyskinesia (limited movement or uncontrolled movement) and Parkinson's-like tremors. There also is raised awareness to their negative effects in cognitive dulling in an educational classroom milieu. Fortunately, in the new class of atypical antipsychotic medications, many of these side effects are of lesser concern. Of more concern are the issues around weight gain and secondary complications of obesity, such as metabolic syndrome or diabetes, which are some of the other possible serious side effects. Antipsychotics thus require close monitoring.

Following is a review of some antipsychotic medications and their use in Asperger's syndrome:

Risperdal (risperidone)   This is most commonly used to treat severe disruptive behaviors, aggression, irritability, impulsivity, repetitive behaviors, and self-injurious behavior. Well-controlled clinical trials and ten to twelve years' worth of data on its efficacy highlight the usefulness of this agent in the above symptoms. However, the drug had absolutely no effect on impaired communication and social interactions.

There is a growing belief that once aggressive and unremitting behaviors are controlled, the child becomes more cognitively available for social interaction, better communication, and learning opportunities. This remains to be determined by a long-term follow-up.

Risperidone has been shown to have sustained efficacy for anywhere from six to eight weeks to approximately a year. The side effects of tardive dyskinesia and Parkinson's-like side effects were found not to be present as often as expected. There are occurrences of transient sedation, tremors, and hypersalivation that improved with the usage of the medication. The significant side effects are an increase in weight and in appetite and, rarely, an increase in the hormone prolactin (the hormone that is usually secreted during the lactation process in women; it can result in the formation of breasts in men).

Aripiprazole (Abilify)   This drug has had recent approval by the FDA and has shown increasing usage in clinical practice. Since 2008, it has been a primary drug of choice in my practice to treat aggression, self-injurious behaviors, and severe temper tantrums. Though sharing the same side effect profile as risperidone, it tends to have a slightly better overall tolerance profile. Used in lower- to medium-dosage range (two to ten milligrams), it has also been shown to stabilize mood and poor frustration tolerance for patients in my practice. Abilify tends to have fewer side effects of weight gain and metabolic syndrome and appears to be fairly benign when it comes to side effects on the heart and its rhythm. This drug, like all antipsychotic medications, requires close monitoring.

Zyprexa (olanzapine) There are several case-study reports and one controlled study showing the efficacy of this drug in the reduction of aggression in patients with autism. It is increasingly used in Asperger's syndrome, especially with comorbid disturbed mood, mania, and/or depression. There is a growing consensus that this is a good alternative when the first-line drug, risperidone, does not work. *However, this drug is not FDA-approved for its specific use in Asperger's syndrome.* No medication has been approved by the FDA for Asperger's. Risperdal and Abilify have approval in autism only. Off-label meds are used to balance risk versus benefit. *All meds used in Asperger's are off-label, irrespective of diagnosis.* Zyprexa showed in one controlled study to benefit aggression in autism, and from there we extrapolate and use it in Asperger's. There have been increasing reports of improvements in social behavior, hyperactivity, anxiety, and depression in many patients. Weight gain and sedation are common side effects and limit the long-term use of this drug. Ethnic minorities, specifically Hispanics and Asians, seem to be a bit more sensitive to the weight gain and metabolic syndrome side effects.

Seroquel (quetiapine) There have been only two open-label studies targeting aggression, irritability, and autism with this medication. There is no evidence that it is beneficial in relieving aggression and irritability. This medication was poorly tolerated and had significant side effects, including sedation, weight gain, increased appetite, behavior activation (symptoms of increased irritability, aggression, lack of sleep, and mood lability), and, in one case, seizure inducement. This medication is therefore not recommended for Asperger's syndrome.

Clozaril (clozapine)   There are a very limited number of studies on the use of this medication. It requires frequent blood monitoring to tackle the issue of agranulocytosis (reduction of the white-blood-cell count), which results with prolonged usage. Frequent blood tests in children with Asperger's syndrome are unrealistic, which thereby severely limits the potential of this medication.

Geodon (ziprasidone)   This drug has had some open-label studies. It targets aggression, irritability, lack of self-control, and self-injurious behavior in Asperger's syndrome. There is a very slight increase in the possibility of side effects related to the rhythmic beat of the heart that limits the drug's use and requires close monitoring. Geodon has been effective in individuals who have failed to respond to risperidone and olanzapine. The drug has shown to be very beneficial for severe tics. It needs to be used in low dosages, about 20 to 40 mg, under close supervision.

Typical antipsychotics   From the 1960s to the 1980s, there was significant use of typical antipsychotic medications, such as Haldol (haloperidol) and Prolixin (fluphenazine). These medications are notorious for the following side effects: sedation, cognitive dulling, increased prolactin, enormous weight gain, tardive dyskinesia, and Parkinson's-like tremors. Their use today is limited, but they are used occasionally, when other medications do not succeed in controlling severe aggression and irritability in children with Asperger's syndrome. They require close monitoring.

Lithium This is a classic mood stabilizer that has been used in many children with Asperger's syndrome and bipolar disorder. It can have negative side effects on the thyroid and kidney functions and therefore requires close monitoring, especially in young children.

Beta-Blockers

Beta-blockers are a class of medication used in cardiology for management of blood pressure. They have found some usage in autistic spectrum disorders to manage anxiety and aggression. Propranolol, atenolol, and metoprolol have been used in the treatment of aggression in individuals with brain injury or brain diseases. There have been a few studies of their use in children with Asperger's syndrome. However, their use is not recommended because of their significant number of side effects.

Sleep Agents

Melatonin is now being used to tackle sleep problems in children with Asperger's syndrome. There are no data that show its clear benefit. However, open-label trials and small case studies have shown encouraging results that support its benefit for people with mental retardation and Asperger's syndrome.

Melatonin produces sleep without causing drowsiness the next day, and it does not create the withdrawal effect of rebound insomnia. The side effects are minimal, but in high dosages it can cause occasional abdominal cramps, fatigue, headache, dizziness, and increased irritability. The dosage range is 1 to 3 mg, with a maximum of 6 mg used on an occasional basis in difficult cases. Melatonin has a very short half-life in the blood. Although it tends to help in inducing sleep, it is not very effective in sustaining or prolonging sleep duration. Though not approved by long-term studies, I have used melatonin along with an anti-epileptic agent, Neurontin, in lower dosages to help sustain sleep throughout the night. It is a medication with a very good overall side effect profile and is beneficial in the treatment of mild anxiety in many individuals with Asperger's syndrome.

Home-to-School Perspective

Behavior is a message from a child to the parents, the peers, the teachers, and the support personnel. Its intent is almost always to indicate a need, a desire, a feeling, or an interaction of some kind. In my (Melinda's) experience, behavior is a form of communication. Children do not repeatedly engage in a particular behavior unless there is a regular payoff—unless, of course, it is an involuntary behavior affiliated with a neurological diagnosis such as Tourette's syndrome. Sometimes the payoff is difficult to determine, but our job as adults is to figure out the need that is being met. It is not always as clear as we would like it to be, so that's where creativity comes into play.

Home-to-School Interventions

In order to change behavior, we need to figure out what need is being met when the child engages in a particular behavior. Here is an example. A certain boy throws a fit in the middle of the classroom, and every person, adult and child, tries to calm him, by asking questions, handing him a toy, distracting him, holding him, taking him away from the situation, or just plain ignoring him. Finally, to the relief of all involved, one of the attempted strategies quiets the boy. Let's go through the possible options. If the following actions result in a positive response, meaning the child is distracted or the aggression wanes, then these would be the possible reasons for the positive result:

- **(Action) "Do you want to play this game with me?"** Possible need for peer or adult interactions.

- **(Action) A child gives the boy a toy.** Possible need for a tangible item, although it could just be the interaction in and of itself.

- **(Action) "Hey, look at what Tommy is doing."** Distraction is a possible intervention, especially if the boy is perseverating on a particular topic or item. This works well only if the distracter is more motivating than the need that is being met by the tantrum.

- **(Action) Putting your arms around the boy or holding him on your lap.** Possible sensory need, such as deep pressure or a feeling of safeness.

- **(Action) Taking him away from the situation.** Possible need for a break; the environment is too stimulating, either from activity or the noise level; need for one-to-one attention; removal from an unpreferred activity.

- **(Action) Active ignoring.** Possible need for the boy to realize that he will not achieve anything positive with inappropriate behavior, so he stops the behavior on his own.

Alternate Appropriate Behaviors That Meet the Same Need

We now need to look at which scenario has calmed the boy in our example and try to prompt him to express that need in a more appropriate way in the future. Let's go through the scenarios again. Your job is to utilize the prior knowledge to create a situation in which you can minimize the inappropriate behavior and meet the boy's needs at the same time. Remember that I have chosen only a few possibilities and that there may be many more.

- **Playing a game.** Set up a classroom environment in which the boy has a choice of an educational game or a preferred topic.
- **Giving the boy a toy.** Provide a choice of toys ahead of time to avoid possible conflict with another child.
- **"Hey, look at what Tommy is doing."** If the distraction is effective because of the interaction, the teacher or parent has to proactively provide additional opportunities for peer interaction, such as playdates, peer centers with highly preferred activities, peer tutoring, and cooperative learning groups. If the distraction is effective because of a preference for the activity Tommy was doing or the toy that Tommy was playing with, then proactive opportunities must be set up to allow more opportunities to engage with this item or in this activity.
- **Putting your arms around the boy or holding him on your lap.** Proactive sensory input, as indicated by an occupational therapist, such as deep pressure and/or squeezes, provides the sensory input that the child is seeking. However, if the need for the physical interaction is simply to provide security, one can achieve that by allowing the boy to hold a stuffed animal, assuming it is age-appropriate, work in small groups to have a close-knit feeling of safety, and/or complete work or take time in a quiet area.
- **Taking him away from the situation.** If this strategy is effective in calming the boy, then one should look at what he was being taken away from: an overstimulating environment, an unpreferred academic topic or chore, or a teacher or parent direction that he dislikes. The teacher or the parent should provide a more appropriate way for the boy to let the adult know that the classroom is too noisy, that he didn't understand the directions, or that he was feeling overwhelmed by the presentation of the academic material.

- **Active ignoring.** Best practices dictate that catching him when he is behaving appropriately and positively reinforcing that appropriate behavior will lead to additional long-lasting appropriate behavior. Therefore, the proactive measures to be taken in this area are to set up an environment for success ahead of time, break chores or academic activities into small chunks, or break up directions into one or two steps rather than relying on the boy to hear, process, and remember a list of instructions. Check for understanding by using synonyms and rephrasing directions rather than simply asking the boy to repeat what you have said.

Our job is to provide a more appropriate way to allow children to get their needs met. This may be achieved by an adult behavior, such as proactively changing the environment or prompting a child to use a set script of words such as "I am angry" or "It's too noisy in here and I need to go outside." If the verbal requirement is too overwhelming for the child, a card or a signal can be put in place to achieve the same effect.

Motivators

There have been times when I've asked a teacher or a parent to tell me what certain children are doing when they are happy, content, and behaving appropriately. Much of the time the answer I receive is either "Nothing" or "They're always misbehaving." This is impossible. All children have times during the day when they are content, happy, and behaving in an appropriate manner. The observant adult needs to identify what the children are doing during that time; then either the environment or the activity becomes the motivator for future appropriate behavior.

There is also an art to scheduling actual educational activities. If children are significantly behavioral, presenting with inappropriate behaviors on a daily basis, you would want to start off with a high-interest activity with a highly preferred adult.

If there are aides, assistants, or therapists who are highly preferred by the children, you would match the most preferred adult to the most preferred activity for each child. Children will have the most motivation with the least bad behaviors with this setup; at least, this is what should happen, in theory.

Ideally, the children will get to the point of understanding that sometimes we have to engage in activities that we do not like and deal with people whom we do not like; many children are far away from that, however. To facilitate the success of less preferred activities with less preferred people, it helps to alternate academic activities that are highly preferred with the not-so-preferred, so that every two or three activities, the children will engage in an activity that they like.

When children approach an activity that is required and nonnegotiable, the adult needs to set up the environment for success with the use of the children's personal motivators. For example, a rule could be set that when they finish five problems of math, they will be allowed to look at their Pokémon cards; when they finish five more problems, they will be allowed to draw for five minutes.

Children with Asperger's syndrome become very overwhelmed at the thought of an enormous assignment, a long task, or a day filled with activities. All of these are more manageable if they are broken into smaller parts, not only for processing but to allow the children to rest in between each part, process the information, and request and allow time for a break.

Positive Behavior Support

I am a firm believer in positive behavior support. Children consistently need to know what they are doing that is positive. If children are consistently positively rewarded for appropriate behavior, and the reward that is given to them is motivating, they will continue doing that behavior.

However, I also believe that there is a time and a place for telling children what they are not allowed to do. For example, when we say, "You should speak appropriately with your peer," children will not always understand what *appropriately* means. It's better if you say, "We should use kind words," "We should be respectful," or "We should say hello." These are examples of appropriate scripts. It is okay, and sometimes very necessary, to tell a child no. However, this should be followed with a reason for the no and with an explanation. Simply saying "Because I said so" will not improve the situation, learning will not take place, and anxiety will most likely increase.

However, just because children learn appropriate verbal interactions does not mean that they also understand that they may not use swear words, call someone a loser, or make faces at other people. Thus, sometimes they not only need a positive behavior support, they also need to be told what they are not allowed to do.

Consequences for Behavior

The objective of changing behavior is to teach good behavior before it turns bad, and this is all a matter of timing. Consequences do play a part in positive behavior support. However, consequences are a bandage; a short-term intervention might stop bad behavior temporarily, but the need to teach is still there. A short-term intervention is not a long-term intervention.

Consequences are useful and temporarily effective if the children have the ability to understand that if they engage in the same behavior again, a similar consequence will follow; for example, "I better not push in line, because the last time I did, I was not allowed to go out for recess."

Most children with Asperger's syndrome are not able to do that. If they were able to process such information, they would not behave as they do. I caution you to be very careful in using consequences. It is a quick, temporary fix for a long-term problem.

Choices

Intervening before appropriate behavior turns inappropriate can be effective with a combination of timing and choices. For example, let's say a certain girl is able to engage in a reasonably preferred activity for seven to eight minutes with minimal adult prompts. However, we know from past experience that if we push her—be it to clean her room, do homework, or rake the leaves— for nine to ten minutes we run the risk of causing a meltdown.

Once the meltdown has occurred, that is not the time to offer her a choice, such as taking a break, because the choice has then been implemented directly after inappropriate behavior, which thereby rewards the inappropriate behavior. The objective is to offer the choice while the child is still engaging in appropriate behavior, before the child begins to escalate. We do not want to wait until she is at the height of her anxiety and then try to get her to use every skill she has ever been taught.

There are many times when we, as adults, can intervene before children become aggressive or violent. Those are the times when you need to prompt the children to take a break and breathe deeply, offer a distraction, give another choice, or take them to a calm place. However, you do not always have the luxury of intervention, and sometimes those episodes just have to run their course, regardless of the interventions that you implement.

You, as the adult, must control your own anxiety. If you respond to children's episodes with your own anxiety, no learning or teaching will take place for the children. If you become agitated, frustrated, or impatient with children, you are actually responding to your own anxiety rather than the children's situation. For example, the louder a child becomes, the quieter you should become. The more agitated a child becomes, the calmer you should become.

Research has shown that giving choices reduces behavioral issues. If children are allowed to choose the order of the tasks they have to do, inappropriate behavior is much less likely. If math is the trigger for a meltdown, allow the child to complete a portion of the assignment, followed by a break or a preferred activity. The same rule applies for homework or a household chore—ten minutes of raking the leaves and five minutes of their desired video game.

Another strategy is to allow children to participate in the order of events. Thus they do not get out of completing their math homework, but they get to choose to have a five-minute break first. This is applicable to both academic and therapeutic environments.

There is no sense engaging in a power struggle with a child, because once you, as the adult, find yourself in that situation, you have already lost. The purpose is to engage children in what will benefit them in the long run in a variety of environments with the least amount of opposition. Ideally, we want our children to be independent and able to stand up for themselves. Participation in making choices that reflect their needs and their wants supports this philosophy.

More about Prediction

As I've already mentioned in previous chapters, predicting what will come next (where we are going, who will be there, how long it will take, how noisy it will be, and what it will look or feel like) reduces a great deal of anxiety in children with Asperger's syndrome and therefore reduces their need to behave inappropriately. The caveat is that just because you predicted that recess would be noisy on a Monday does not mean that you won't have to do it again on Tuesday. It does not mean that just because you have reminded your child every Sunday that Aunt Mabel hugs too tight and smells funny doesn't mean that your child will remember it the next Sunday.

Predicting is, without a doubt, the single most effective strategy to help children feel more comfortable in an environment, feel safe and less anxious, and allow teachable moments to occur. However, the strategy is not a once-in-awhile intervention. It will not be effective if it is implemented haphazardly. It must be done every day—before, during, and after every activity with every teacher, every therapist, every service provider, and every family member.

This doesn't mean that the world will come to an end if you forget. Just keep in mind that for every time you are able to implement the strategy, many situations go by that were not tended to, which therefore leave you with the need to make up for those moments.

Zachary did eventually get to the point where his need for predicting is minimal, if at all. The bigger picture must also include the teaching of coping skills if the need for predicting is still there but doesn't happen. If you teach the coping strategies along with the long-term increase in flexibility, you should have successes along the way.

Clarification of Expectations

We all want to know what is expected of us, whether that is in a classroom, as part of a family, or as an employee. Children with Asperger's syndrome especially need to have this kind of road map to guide them through the world of unknown and possibly terrifying thoughts and experiences.

Expectations should foster success. They should be just challenging enough to foster motivation within a child, but not so overwhelming that the child gives up without even attempting the task.

The trick is to determine the fine line of motivating versus overwhelming; this is determined through the perception of the child, not your own. Just because you think your child or your student should be able to do at least five math problems because everyone else is doing ten doesn't mean that you won't have to reduce the requirement yet again to three problems.

The objective is success while increasing self-esteem and self-confidence. This can be achieved only if the child feels safe enough to attempt the task and is successful several times.

Erring on the side of caution is much better than requiring an expectation that cannot be met. This holds true for expectations of schoolwork, peer interactions, family functions, household chores, and any other situation.

Consistent and Continual Reminders

Many children with Asperger's syndrome have difficulties with auditory processing and short-term memory recall. Once again, we want to facilitate success in a safe, nurturing environment, not see how long a child can remember a direction that has been given only once.

However, that being said, we also want to foster independence and responsibility, which is where verbal and visual cues come in. Parents and educators should provide the most support possible, such as visual schedules and verbal reminders, as often as necessary. As a child becomes accustomed to a routine and the expectations for a particular activity, assignment, or social situation, we can begin to reduce the amount of verbal reminders or visual cues. This must be done slowly, carefully, one at a time, and we must take great care to determine that at every step of the way the child feels successful, safe, and supported.

Immediate Reinforcement

Immediately reinforcing expected behavior by utilizing an individualized reinforcement plan lets children know that they are on the right track. Everyone loves positive reinforcement, and our kids need it several times a day; some need it several times a minute, which is why it must be individualized. The reinforcement must be motivating to each particular child, or it will not be effective. The high-five and the warm smile that work wonders for one might go unnoticed by a child who responds to a sticker. This is applicable to the classroom, the therapeutic environment, and the home.

13

Current Research in
Neuroimaging

Neuroimaging, magnetic resonance imaging (MRI), CT scans, and various other imaging techniques have a research value in Asperger's syndrome, but they still lack clinical application. However, current data support the clinical use of neuroimaging in children with autism, and some of this data is being extrapolated for use in Asperger's syndrome. The following review is primarily of the neuroimaging done recently in the field of autistic spectrum disorder, some of which has applicability providing clarity in Asperger's syndrome.

MRIs have been used to explore the cause of large heads in children with autism. In spite of being born with a normal head circumference, 30 percent of children with autism have an eventual increase in head growth. Several researchers have noted that this seems to happen by the time the child is about one year old.

Many of the infants with large heads are low-functioning, have an increased incidence of seizures, and suffer from many behavioral problems.

One study was done by Joseph Piven of the University of North Carolina. He examined the brain volume and head circumference of children with autism and compared these figures with those of normal control subjects. The primary objective was to determine at what point in development the brain began to enlarge as well as the type of enlargement of the brain. This study compared children with autism between ages of eighteen and thirty-five months to a control group of typically developing children from birth to three years of age. The researchers measured the thickness of the brain and the size of the gray matter, and studied the cerebellum.

The findings were quite significant. Until one year of age, there was no difference between the brain of a child with autism and the brain of a normally developed child. However, the head circumference started enlarging in children with autism after one year. The most significant finding was the growth in the gray and the white matter of the brain; this was responsible for the large size. Identification before early toddlerhood can generate an array of interventions to prevent some of the challenges faced by these children.

Another area of interest has been to study the network of the prefrontal and parietal areas of the brain in children with Asperger's syndrome. It has been known for a long time that children with Asperger's syndrome have quite normal visual-spatial abilities, but they tend to lag behind in executive functioning, especially in areas of attention and working memory.

In order to explore some of these issues through neuroimaging, a study was conducted in Australia that showed that Asperger's syndrome individuals showed much less activation than the control subjects in the lateral and the medial parts of the premotor cortex, the dorsal-lateral prefrontal cortex, the anterior cingulate gyrus, and the caudate nucleus areas of the brain. These are the areas that are primarily responsible for executive functioning. Medications that target these areas and clearly correlate with clinical improvement remain a challenge.

If Asperger's syndrome were, in fact, a true genetic disorder, the unaffected parents of children with the condition would have similar brain abnormalities. Some studies have shown that 5 percent of the unaffected parents had brain abnormalities.

However, a comprehensive study done in the Netherlands showed no such difference. Using an MRI on the unaffected parents of nineteen autistic children, the researchers studied intracranial total brain volume; the frontal, parietal, temporal, and occipital lobes; the cerebral and cortical gray matter; the white matter; the cerebellum; and the lateral and third ventricles. There was, much to their surprise, no significant difference found between the parents of autistic children and healthy control couples with normal children.

Even when the sex of the child and the parent was added as a variable in the study, nothing was revealed. This led to the conclusion that unaffected parents of children with autism do not show brain enlargement or intracranium enlargement, and their structures are well within normal levels.

This raises an important question about the supposed genetic origins of autism. Is it possible that an interaction of paternal and maternal genes combines with environmental factors to cause the increased brain volume that is seen in children with autism?

The effect of face and voice reading, neuronal correlations, and communication patterns in adolescents with Asperger's syndrome are other areas of neuroimaging study. There is an established clinical understanding that children with Asperger's syndrome have abnormalities in the understanding of conversational language. This may be related to an inability to read social cues, such as facial expression and tone and vocal timbre, cadence, and pitch. Several studies have shown reduced activity in the brain region that responds selectively to the face and the voice.

In order to examine this neurocircuitry in detail and interpret the communicative intention through concepts such as comprehension, humor, and irony, a study at the UCLA Department of Psychiatry compared the brains of eighteen typically developing boys with the brains of eighteen boys diagnosed with Asperger's syndrome. The blood oxygenation level of the brain was measured during the presentation of short scenarios involving irony. The behaviors of the individuals were also recorded. Reduced prefrontal cortex activity directly correlated to the inability to decipher irony. This is an exciting field of inquiry for the future.

Approximately 25 to 40 percent of children with autism have a seizure disorder. Researchers have examined the cortical thickness of the brain from postmortem studies of individuals with autism who died natural deaths. A study at Stanford University of seventeen children looked specifically for the sulcal (groove) depth and the thickness of the brain and its lobes. Clear evidence of increased cortical thickness was seen; this contributes to the gray-matter volume and the total brain size, which have already been observed in autism. The enlarged size of the brain might lead to abnormal connections, thereby explaining the high incidence of seizures, and an abnormal surface area might lead to poor electrical-chemical conduction in various areas of the brain.

In imaging studies, a growing interest is developing in the differences between women and men suffering from autism spectrum disorder. MRI studies in Britain have shown that women with autism have a smaller density of gray matter in the frontal-temporal areas and the limbic system of the brain compared to men suffering from autism They also have abnormalities in the white matter of the brain, the temporal lobes, and the pons area of the brain.

Eric Courchesne in San Diego looked at the neuroanatomy of young girls with autism in a preliminary study in 2006. He studied the lobes, the cerebrum, the cerebellum, and brain volume in nine girls with autism, and compared the results to twenty-seven boys with autism and fourteen girls of typical development.

A thorough assessment of the size and the age was done in the age range of four to five years.

He found that the girls exhibited associated abnormalities the same as the boys did. However, additional abnormalities were noted in the girls, including enlargement of the temporal white and gray matter and increased brain volume, related to age. This highlights different anatomical issues in the sexes in autism, and it could have significant treatment implications.

One more interest has been the caudate nucleus area of the brain, which is primarily responsible for working memory. Mount Sinai Hospital conducted neuroimaging studies of the anterior cingulated cortex, the dorsal-striatal thalamic areas, and the caudate nucleus. The MRI and SPET-MRI (single photon emission tomography) coregistration studies showed lower metabolic activity in the caudate area, especially in Asperger's syndrome, thereby highlighting the deficits in working memory in Asperger's syndrome. The imaging studies might open the doors in the future for understanding the pathiophysiology and for developing mechanisms for future treatment.

The lack of social interaction characteristically seen in people with Asperger's syndrome might be caused by the malfunctioning of the frontal-striatal reward system of the brain. No brain imaging studies had been done prior to January 2008 by the Declan GM group in the Netherlands. Declan Group focuses on brain imaging studies, led by a psychiatrist in the field of autism research. The researchers showed that individuals with autism had greater brain activity than the control subjects in the left anterior cingulate gyrus, and this correlated to deficits in social interaction, as measured by a diagnostic interview. It was concluded that the less activity within the cingulated gyrus, which is responsible for attention and arousal, the less social interaction. The cingulated gyrus is associated with the activation of areas known to be responsible for attention and arousal, and this may partially explain some deficits in social behavior.

The amygdala is another important area of the brain that has been the subject of imaging investigations. Deficits in amygdala size have been hypothesized to be related to abnormalities in understanding nonverbal social cues. A group in Madison, Wisconsin, studied abnormal social behavior and tried to link it with amygdala volume in individuals with Asperger's syndrome. They showed that the volume abnormalities in the amygdala were related to deficits in reading facial expressions and eye tracking. Individuals with Asperger's syndrome who have a smaller amygdala show a lack of fixation on others' eyes, which is imperative for social interaction. This is an exciting study and this needs further exploration.

Studies done in Seattle, Washington, have also looked at the amygdala and the issues of behavioral development. They have shown that three- to four-year-old children with a larger right but not left amygdala had poor socialization and worse outcomes at six years old.

All these new imaging studies are leading to the possibility of early detection and an explanation of many deficits in Asperger's syndrome. This may lead to new developments in treatment in the areas of applied behavior analysis and psychopharmacology.

Appendix

Forms and Templates

This section presents six useful forms that are flexible enough to respond to many situations. We have provided multiple copies of each form, but you should make additional copies as needed so you always have one handy when you have a doctor's appointment or when you meet with teachers, providers, or parents.

The **Student Information Sheet** provides basic information and should be given to teachers and to any new provider, such as a speech-and-language pathologist, an occupational therapist or a psychologist, providing counseling. Whenever basic information changes, updated forms should be provided to all who need them.

Team Meeting Notes can be used to document meetings with providers, teachers, therapists, and other professionals.

The **Autistic Spectrum Disorder Intake Summary** can be used by a professional in a position to diagnose or by a school for initial intake information. This gives a description of the student's baseline and developmental milestones. It can provide valuable information for physicians and treatment teams and can be used to provide additional information to receive an accurate diagnosis early on rather than having the child move from professional to professional before receiving a correct diagnosis.

The **Behavior Tally Sheet** is used to collect data on any targeted behavior. The tallies indicate how many times a behavior occurred during a particular time frame. This information provides not only frequency but patterns related to when the behavior occurs. It can be used by the parent, the classroom teacher, or the service provider. The information can then be used to create a behavior support plan or to give meaningful information to team members so they are able to revise their treatment plans.

The **Antecedent—Behavior—Consequence (ABC) Data Sheet** is specifically used to document patterns in behavior. It will enable you to recognize the time of the behavior, the antecedent (that is, what happened directly before the behavior), the actual behavior, and its consequence. The recommended time for use of this form is ten days. This time frame will give the user enough data to determine if there are any patterns of antecedents causing a particular behavior or consequences/responses that are effective or that make the behavior worse. Upon completion, you will determine by the child's response to the consequence whether the consequence you chose was effective. If it was, continue. If it was not, you need to revise your approach. This form is useful for all providers, professionals, and parents who are trying to document behavior.

Once an adequate amount of data has been collected, it will be used to complete the **Behavior Support Plan**. All teams members should agree to this plan and implement consistent strategies notated on the form.

Student Information Sheet

Last name:	First name:	Date of birth:	Diagnosis/Eligibility:
Date annual Individualized Education Plan is due:		Transportation:	Classroom teacher:
Date 3-year Individualized Education Plan is due:		Classroom #:	

Parent Contact Information

	Mother	Father
Name:		
Address:		
Phone:		
E-mail:		
Emergency number:		

Medical Information

Current medications:	Current medications administered during school:	Allergies: ☐ Yes ☐ No (Please describe any food or medication allergies and list the side effects for each item.)
Time of day medications are administered:		

153

Student Information Sheet *(continued)*

Triggers:	Calming strategies:	Additional information:

Summary of objectives:	Accommodations:	Related services/Minutes:

Medication Log

Medication trials: How many times was it tried?	Dose prescribed:	Side effects of medication trial:

Student Information Sheet

Last name:	First name:	Date of birth:	Diagnosis/Eligibility:
Date annual Individualized Education Plan is due:		Transportation:	Classroom teacher:
Date 3-year Individualized Education Plan is due:		Classroom #:	

Parent Contact Information

	Mother	Father
Name:		
Address:		
Phone:		
E-mail:		
Emergency number:		

Medical Information

Current medications:	Current medications administered during school:	Allergies: ☐ Yes ☐ No (Please describe any food or medication allergies and list the side effects for each item.)
Time of day medications are administered:		

155

Student Information Sheet *(continued)*

Triggers:	Calming strategies:	Additional information:

Summary of objectives:	Accommodations:	Related services/Minutes:

Medication Log

Medication trials: How many times was it tried?	Dose prescribed:	Side effects of medication trial:

Student Information Sheet

Last name:	First name:	Date of birth:	Diagnosis/Eligibility:
Date annual Individualized Education Plan is due:		Transportation:	Classroom teacher:
Date 3-year Individualized Education Plan is due:		Classroom #:	

Parent Contact Information

	Mother	Father
Name:		
Address:		
Phone:		
E-mail:		
Emergency number:		

Medical Information

Current medications:	Current medications administered during school:	Allergies: ☐ Yes ☐ No (Please describe any food or medication allergies and list the side effects for each item.)
Time of day medications are administered:		

Student Information Sheet *(continued)*

Triggers:	Calming strategies:	Additional information:

Summary of objectives:	Accommodations:	Related services/Minutes:

Medication Log

Medication trials: How many times was it tried?	Dose prescribed:	Side effects of medication trial:

Student Information Sheet

Last name:	First name:	Date of birth:	Diagnosis/Eligibility:
Date annual Individualized Education Plan is due:		Transportation:	Classroom teacher:
Date 3-year Individualized Education Plan is due:		Classroom #:	

Parent Contact Information

	Mother	Father
Name:		
Address:		
Phone:		
E-mail:		
Emergency number:		

Medical Information

Current medications:	Current medications administered during school:	Allergies: ☐ Yes ☐ No (Please describe any food or medication allergies and list the side effects for each item.)
Time of day medications are administered:		

Student Information Sheet *(continued)*

Triggers:	Calming strategies:	Additional information:

Summary of objectives:	Accommodations:	Related services/Minutes:

Medication Log

Medication trials: How many times was it tried?	Dose prescribed:	Side effects of medication trial:

Student Information Sheet

Last name:	First name:	Date of birth:	Diagnosis/Eligibility:
Date annual Individualized Education Plan is due:		Transportation:	Classroom teacher:
Date 3-year Individualized Education Plan is due:		Classroom #:	

Parent Contact Information

	Mother	Father
Name:		
Address:		
Phone:		
E-mail:		
Emergency number:		

Medical Information

Current medications:	Current medications administered during school:	Allergies: ☐ Yes ☐ No (Please describe any food or medication allergies and list the side effects for each item.)
Time of day medications are administered:		

Student Information Sheet *(continued)*

Triggers:	Calming strategies:	Additional information:

Summary of objectives:	Accommodations:	Related services/Minutes:

Medication Log

Medication trials: How many times was it tried?	Dose prescribed:	Side effects of medication trial:

Student Information Sheet

Last name:	First name:	Date of birth:	Diagnosis/Eligibility:
Date annual Individualized Education Plan is due:		Transportation:	Classroom teacher:
Date 3-year Individualized Education Plan is due:		Classroom #:	

Parent Contact Information

	Mother	Father
Name:		
Address:		
Phone:		
E-mail:		
Emergency number:		

Medical Information

Current medications:	Current medications administered during school:	Allergies: ☐ Yes ☐ No (Please describe any food or medication allergies and list the side effects for each item.)
Time of day medications are administered:		

Student Information Sheet *(continued)*

Triggers:	Calming strategies:	Additional information:

Summary of objectives:	Accommodations:	Related services/Minutes:

Medication Log

Medication trials: How many times was it tried?	Dose prescribed:	Side effects of medication trial:

Student Information Sheet

Last name:	First name:	Date of birth:	Diagnosis/Eligibility:
Date annual Individualized Education Plan is due:		Transportation:	Classroom teacher:
Date 3-year Individualized Education Plan is due:		Classroom #:	

Parent Contact Information

	Mother	Father
Name:		
Address:		
Phone:		
E-mail:		
Emergency number:		

Medical Information

Current medications:	Current medications administered during school:	Allergies: ☐ Yes ☐ No (Please describe any food or medication allergies and list the side effects for each item.)
Time of day medications are administered:		

Student Information Sheet *(continued)*

Triggers:	Calming strategies:	Additional information:

Summary of objectives:	Accommodations:	Related services/Minutes:

Medication Log

Medication trials: How many times was it tried?	Dose prescribed:	Side effects of medication trial:

Team Meeting Notes

Team Meeting for: _____ **Date:** _____

Focus of Discussion: (Check all that apply)

☐ Attendance
☐ Academics
☐ Self-help
☐ Medical concerns
☐ Transportation
☐ Behavior
☐ Related services
☐ Individualized Education Plan goals
☐ Academics
☐ Social skills
☐ Communication
☐ Other (Please explain.):

_____

_____

Strengths/Improvements

Areas of concern

Actions to be taken

Person responsible for monitoring follow-through

Team Meeting Notes

Team Meeting for: _____ **Date:** _____

Focus of Discussion: (Check all that apply)

☐ Attendance
☐ Academics
☐ Self-help
☐ Medical concerns
☐ Transportation
☐ Behavior
☐ Related services
☐ Individualized Education Plan goals
☐ Academics
☐ Social skills
☐ Communication
☐ Other (Please explain.):

_____

_____

Strengths/Improvements

Areas of concern

Actions to be taken

Person responsible for monitoring follow-through

Team Meeting Notes

Team Meeting for: _____   **Date:** _____

Focus of Discussion: (Check all that apply)

- ☐ Attendance
- ☐ Academics
- ☐ Self-help
- ☐ Medical concerns
- ☐ Transportation
- ☐ Behavior
- ☐ Related services
- ☐ Individualized Education Plan goals
- ☐ Academics
- ☐ Social skills
- ☐ Communication
- ☐ Other (Please explain.):

_____

_____

Strengths/Improvements

_____

_____

Areas of concern

_____

_____

Actions to be taken

_____

_____

Person responsible for monitoring follow-through

_____

_____

Team Meeting Notes

Team Meeting for: _____ **Date:** _____

Focus of Discussion: (Check all that apply)

☐ Attendance

☐ Academics

☐ Self-help

☐ Medical concerns

☐ Transportation

☐ Behavior

☐ Related services

☐ Individualized Education Plan goals

☐ Academics

☐ Social skills

☐ Communication

☐ Other (Please explain.):

_____

_____

Strengths/Improvements

Areas of concern

Actions to be taken

Person responsible for monitoring follow-through

Team Meeting Notes

Team Meeting for: _____ **Date:** _____

Focus of Discussion: (Check all that apply)

- ☐ Attendance
- ☐ Academics
- ☐ Self-help
- ☐ Medical concerns
- ☐ Transportation
- ☐ Behavior
- ☐ Related services
- ☐ Individualized Education Plan goals
- ☐ Academics
- ☐ Social skills
- ☐ Communication
- ☐ Other (Please explain.):

_____

_____

Strengths/Improvements

Areas of concern

Actions to be taken

Person responsible for monitoring follow-through

Team Meeting Notes

Team Meeting for: _____ **Date:** _____

Focus of Discussion: (Check all that apply)

☐ Attendance
☐ Academics
☐ Self-help
☐ Medical concerns
☐ Transportation
☐ Behavior
☐ Related services
☐ Individualized Education Plan goals
☐ Academics
☐ Social skills
☐ Communication
☐ Other (Please explain.):

_____

_____

Strengths/Improvements

_____
_____
_____

Areas of concern

_____
_____
_____

Actions to be taken

_____
_____
_____

Person responsible for monitoring follow-through

_____
_____
_____

Team Meeting Notes

Team Meeting for: _____ **Date:** _____

Focus of Discussion: (Check all that apply)

☐ Attendance
☐ Academics
☐ Self-help
☐ Medical concerns
☐ Transportation
☐ Behavior
☐ Related services
☐ Individualized Education Plan goals
☐ Academics
☐ Social skills
☐ Communication
☐ Other (Please explain.):

_____

_____

Strengths/Improvements

Areas of concern

Actions to be taken

Person responsible for monitoring follow-through

Autistic Spectrum Disorder Intake Summary

Date:

Name of student:

Address and contact number:

Birthdate:

School currently attending:

Grade:

Current placement (functional or academic):

Current diagnosis:

Names of parents:

Developmental Information

Did your child develop language before the age of three?

How many words does your child put together to convey a message?

How does your child indicate his wants and needs? (For example: pointing, screaming, grabbing)

Did your child meet other developmental milestones such as sitting, crawling, walking, and pointing to objects?

Is your child able to take care of his/her self-help skills such as putting on clothes, eating, going to the bathroom, brushing teeth, and washing hands, or does he/she need adult assistance?

Autistic Spectrum Disorder Intake Summary

Date:

Name of student:

Address and contact number:

Birthdate:

School currently attending:

Grade:

Current placement (functional or academic):

Current diagnosis:

Names of parents:

Developmental Information

Did your child develop language before the age of three?

How many words does your child put together to convey a message?

How does your child indicate his wants and needs? (For example: pointing, screaming, grabbing)

Did your child meet other developmental milestones such as sitting, crawling, walking, and pointing to objects?

Is your child able to take care of his/her self-help skills such as putting on clothes, eating, going to the bathroom, brushing teeth, and washing hands, or does he/she need adult assistance?

Autistic Spectrum Disorder Intake Summary

Date:

Name of student:

Address and contact number:

Birthdate:

School currently attending:

Grade:

Current placement (functional or academic):

Current diagnosis:

Names of parents:

Developmental Information

Did your child develop language before the age of three?

How many words does your child put together to convey a message?

How does your child indicate his wants and needs? (For example: pointing, screaming, grabbing)

Did your child meet other developmental milestones such as sitting, crawling, walking, and pointing to objects?

Is your child able to take care of his/her self-help skills such as putting on clothes, eating, going to the bathroom, brushing teeth, and washing hands, or does he/she need adult assistance?

Autistic Spectrum Disorder Intake Summary

Date:

Name of student:

Address and contact number:

Birthdate:

School currently attending:

Grade:

Current placement (functional or academic):

Current diagnosis:

Names of parents:

Developmental Information

Did your child develop language before the age of three?

How many words does your child put together to convey a message?

How does your child indicate his wants and needs? (For example: pointing, screaming, grabbing)

Did your child meet other developmental milestones such as sitting, crawling, walking, and pointing to objects?

Is your child able to take care of his/her self-help skills such as putting on clothes, eating, going to the bathroom, brushing teeth, and washing hands, or does he/she need adult assistance?

Autistic Spectrum Disorder Intake Summary

Date:

Name of student:

Address and contact number:

Birthdate:

School currently attending:

Grade:

Current placement (functional or academic):

Current diagnosis:

Names of parents:

Developmental Information

Did your child develop language before the age of three?

How many words does your child put together to convey a message?

How does your child indicate his wants and needs? (For example: pointing, screaming, grabbing)

Did your child meet other developmental milestones such as sitting, crawling, walking, and pointing to objects?

Is your child able to take care of his/her self-help skills such as putting on clothes, eating, going to the bathroom, brushing teeth, and washing hands, or does he/she need adult assistance?

Autistic Spectrum Disorder Intake Summary

Date:

Name of student:

Address and contact number:

Birthdate:

School currently attending:

Grade:

Current placement (functional or academic):

Current diagnosis:

Names of parents:

Developmental Information

Did your child develop language before the age of three?

How many words does your child put together to convey a message?

How does your child indicate his wants and needs? (For example: pointing, screaming, grabbing)

Did your child meet other developmental milestones such as sitting, crawling, walking, and pointing to objects?

Is your child able to take care of his/her self-help skills such as putting on clothes, eating, going to the bathroom, brushing teeth, and washing hands, or does he/she need adult assistance?

Autistic Spectrum Disorder Intake Summary

Date:

Name of student:

Address and contact number:

Birthdate:

School currently attending:

Grade:

Current placement (functional or academic):

Current diagnosis:

Names of parents:

Developmental Information

Did your child develop language before the age of three?

How many words does your child put together to convey a message?

How does your child indicate his wants and needs? (For example: pointing, screaming, grabbing)

Did your child meet other developmental milestones such as sitting, crawling, walking, and pointing to objects?

Is your child able to take care of his/her self-help skills such as putting on clothes, eating, going to the bathroom, brushing teeth, and washing hands, or does he/she need adult assistance?

Behavior Tally Sheet

	Behavior 1	Behavior 2	Activity	Adult with Child
8:00–8:15				
8:15–8:30				
8:30–8:45				
8:45–9:00				
9:00–9:15				
9:15–9:30				
9:30–9:45				
9:45–10:00				
10:00–10:15				
10:15–10:30				
10:30–10:45				
10:45–11:00				
11:00–11:15				
11:15–11:30				
11:30–11:45				
11:45–12:00				
12:00–12:15				
12:15–12:30				
12:30–12:45				
12:45–1:00				
1:00–1:15				
1:15–1:30				
1:30–1:45				
1:45–2:00				
2:00–2:15				
2:15–2:30				

1 Choose one or two target behaviors and identify them at the top of the chart.
2. Use tally marks to document a particular behavior at a particular time.
3. Document activity taking place during behavior.
4. Document adult with the child when the behavior occurred.

Behavior Tally Sheet

	Behavior 1	Behavior 2	Activity	Adult with Child
8:00–8:15				
8:15–8:30				
8:30–8:45				
8:45–9:00				
9:00–9:15				
9:15–9:30				
9:30–9:45				
9:45–10:00				
10:00–10:15				
10:15–10:30				
10:30–10:45				
10:45–11:00				
11:00–11:15				
11:15–11:30				
11:30–11:45				
11:45–12:00				
12:00–12:15				
12:15–12:30				
12:30–12:45				
12:45–1:00				
1:00–1:15				
1:15–1:30				
1:30–1:45				
1:45–2:00				
2:00–2:15				
2:15–2:30				

1 Choose one or two target behaviors and identify them at the top of the chart.
2. Use tally marks to document a particular behavior at a particular time.
3. Document activity taking place during behavior.
4. Document adult with the child when the behavior occurred.

Behavior Tally Sheet

	Behavior 1	Behavior 2	Activity	Adult with Child
8:00–8:15				
8:15–8:30				
8:30–8:45				
8:45–9:00				
9:00–9:15				
9:15–9:30				
9:30–9:45				
9:45–10:00				
10:00–10:15				
10:15–10:30				
10:30–10:45				
10:45–11:00				
11:00–11:15				
11:15–11:30				
11:30–11:45				
11:45–12:00				
12:00–12:15				
12:15–12:30				
12:30–12:45				
12:45–1:00				
1:00–1:15				
1:15–1:30				
1:30–1:45				
1:45–2:00				
2:00–2:15				
2:15–2:30				

1 Choose one or two target behaviors and identify them at the top of the chart.
2. Use tally marks to document a particular behavior at a particular time.
3. Document activity taking place during behavior.
4. Document adult with the child when the behavior occurred.

Behavior Tally Sheet

	Behavior 1	Behavior 2	Activity	Adult with Child
8:00–8:15				
8:15–8:30				
8:30–8:45				
8:45–9:00				
9:00–9:15				
9:15–9:30				
9:30–9:45				
9:45–10:00				
10:00–10:15				
10:15–10:30				
10:30–10:45				
10:45–11:00				
11:00–11:15				
11:15–11:30				
11:30–11:45				
11:45–12:00				
12:00–12:15				
12:15–12:30				
12:30–12:45				
12:45–1:00				
1:00–1:15				
1:15–1:30				
1:30–1:45				
1:45–2:00				
2:00–2:15				
2:15–2:30				

1. Choose one or two target behaviors and identify them at the top of the chart.
2. Use tally marks to document a particular behavior at a particular time.
3. Document activity taking place during behavior.
4. Document adult with the child when the behavior occurred.

Behavior Tally Sheet

	Behavior 1	Behavior 2	Activity	Adult with Child
8:00–8:15				
8:15–8:30				
8:30–8:45				
8:45–9:00				
9:00–9:15				
9:15–9:30				
9:30–9:45				
9:45–10:00				
10:00–10:15				
10:15–10:30				
10:30–10:45				
10:45–11:00				
11:00–11:15				
11:15–11:30				
11:30–11:45				
11:45–12:00				
12:00–12:15				
12:15–12:30				
12:30–12:45				
12:45–1:00				
1:00–1:15				
1:15–1:30				
1:30–1:45				
1:45–2:00				
2:00–2:15				
2:15–2:30				

1. Choose one or two target behaviors and identify them at the top of the chart.
2. Use tally marks to document a particular behavior at a particular time.
3. Document activity taking place during behavior.
4. Document adult with the child when the behavior occurred.

Behavior Tally Sheet

	Behavior 1	Behavior 2	Activity	Adult with Child
8:00–8:15				
8:15–8:30				
8:30–8:45				
8:45–9:00				
9:00–9:15				
9:15–9:30				
9:30–9:45				
9:45–10:00				
10:00–10:15				
10:15–10:30				
10:30–10:45				
10:45–11:00				
11:00–11:15				
11:15–11:30				
11:30–11:45				
11:45–12:00				
12:00–12:15				
12:15–12:30				
12:30–12:45				
12:45–1:00				
1:00–1:15				
1:15–1:30				
1:30–1:45				
1:45–2:00				
2:00–2:15				
2:15–2:30				

1 Choose one or two target behaviors and identify them at the top of the chart.
2. Use tally marks to document a particular behavior at a particular time.
3. Document activity taking place during behavior.
4. Document adult with the child when the behavior occurred.

Behavior Tally Sheet

	Behavior 1	Behavior 2	Activity	Adult with Child
8:00–8:15				
8:15–8:30				
8:30–8:45				
8:45–9:00				
9:00–9:15				
9:15–9:30				
9:30–9:45				
9:45–10:00				
10:00–10:15				
10:15–10:30				
10:30–10:45				
10:45–11:00				
11:00–11:15				
11:15–11:30				
11:30–11:45				
11:45–12:00				
12:00–12:15				
12:15–12:30				
12:30–12:45				
12:45–1:00				
1:00–1:15				
1:15–1:30				
1:30–1:45				
1:45–2:00				
2:00–2:15				
2:15–2:30				

1 Choose one or two target behaviors and identify them at the top of the chart.
2. Use tally marks to document a particular behavior at a particular time.
3. Document activity taking place during behavior.
4. Document adult with the child when the behavior occurred.

Antecedent—Behavior—Consequence Data Sheet

Student's Name:

Targeted Behavior:

Date	Time of Day	Antecedent	Behavior	Consequence	Adult's Initials
		(Describe what happened before the behavior occurred, including the activity and the setting.) Activity: Setting:	(What did the child do? Describe in detail. Example: Stamped feet, screamed, and ran around the room for five minutes.) ☐ mild ☐ moderate ☐ severe	(Describe what happened after the behavior, including how staff responded to it.) Staff's response: Child's response: ☐ ignore ☐ escalate ☐ de-escalate	

Antecedent—Behavior—Consequence Data Sheet

Student's Name:

Targeted Behavior:

Date	Time of Day	Antecedent	Behavior	Consequence	Adult's Initials
		(Describe what happened before the behavior occurred, including the activity and the setting.) Activity: Setting:	(What did the child do? Describe in detail. Example: Stamped feet, screamed, and ran around the room for five minutes.) ☐ mild ☐ moderate ☐ severe	(Describe what happened after the behavior, including how staff responded to it.) Staff's response: Child's response: ☐ ignore ☐ escalate ☐ de-escalate	

Antecedent—Behavior—Consequence Data Sheet

Student's Name:

Targeted Behavior:

Date	Time of Day	Antecedent	Behavior	Consequence	Adult's Initials
		(Describe what happened before the behavior occurred, including the activity and the setting.) Activity: Setting:	(What did the child do? Describe in detail. Example: Stamped feet, screamed, and ran around the room for five minutes.) ☐ mild ☐ moderate ☐ severe	(Describe what happened after the behavior, including how staff responded to it.) Staff's response: Child's response: ☐ ignore ☐ escalate ☐ de-escalate	

Antecedent—Behavior—Consequence Data Sheet

Student's Name:

Targeted Behavior:

Date	Time of Day	Antecedent	Behavior	Consequence	Adult's Initials
		(Describe what happened before the behavior occurred, including the activity and the setting.) Activity: Setting:	(What did the child do? Describe in detail. Example: Stamped feet, screamed, and ran around the room for five minutes.) ☐ mild ☐ moderate ☐ severe	(Describe what happened after the behavior, including how staff responded to it.) Staff's response: Child's response: ☐ ignore ☐ escalate ☐ de-escalate	

Antecedent—Behavior—Consequence Data Sheet

Student's Name:

Targeted Behavior:

Date	Time of Day	Antecedent	Behavior	Consequence	Adult's Initials
		(Describe what happened before the behavior occurred, including the activity and the setting.) Activity: Setting:	(What did the child do? Describe in detail. Example: Stamped feet, screamed, and ran around the room for five minutes.) ☐ mild ☐ moderate ☐ severe	(Describe what happened after the behavior, including how staff responded to it.) Staff's response: Child's response: ☐ ignore ☐ escalate ☐ de-escalate	

Antecedent—Behavior—Consequence Data Sheet

Student's Name: **Targeted Behavior:**

Date	Time of Day	Antecedent	Behavior	Consequence	Adult's Initials
		(Describe what happened before the behavior occurred, including the activity and the setting.) Activity: Setting:	(What did the child do? Describe in detail. Example: Stamped feet, screamed, and ran around the room for five minutes.) ☐ mild ☐ moderate ☐ severe	(Describe what happened after the behavior, including how staff responded to it.) Staff's response: Child's response: ☐ ignore ☐ escalate ☐ de-escalate	

Antecedent—Behavior—Consequence Data Sheet

Student's Name:

Targeted Behavior:

Date	Time of Day	Antecedent	Behavior	Consequence	Adult's Initials
		(Describe what happened before the behavior occurred, including the activity and the setting.) Activity: Setting:	(What did the child do? Describe in detail. Example: Stamped feet, screamed, and ran around the room for five minutes.) ☐ mild ☐ moderate ☐ severe	(Describe what happened after the behavior, including how staff responded to it.) Staff's response: Child's response: ☐ ignore ☐ escalate ☐ de-escalate	

Behavior Support Plan

Date:

Name of student:

Review plan by:

1. Describe the behavior, including frequency.

2. What occurred directly before the behavior?

3. What occurred after the behavior?

4. When does the behavior occur? (For example, during transitional periods such as before and after activities, during particular activities)

5. Where does the behavior occur? (Give location and activity.)

6. Who is present/absent when the behavior occurs?

7. What is the reason for the behavior? What purpose does the behavior serve for the student? (for example, a sensory need, the desire to escape or avoid an activity or a person, a need for attention, or a desire for a tangible object.)

8. Identify alternate behaviors that could serve the same purpose.

9. Provide reinforcement strategies to support student learning, including verbal praise, desired tangible items, a choice of preferred item or activity, and free time.

10. Provide modifications and support in the school/classroom environment, such as verbal cues, preparing for transitions, picture schedules, choices, rewrite assignments to reduce unnecessary material on a page and/or to reduce the amount of questions or problems.

Behavior Support Plan

Date:

Name of student:

Review plan by:

1. Describe the behavior, including frequency.

2. What occurred directly before the behavior?

3. What occurred after the behavior?

4. When does the behavior occur? (For example, during transitional periods such as before and after activities, during particular activities)

5. Where does the behavior occur? (Give location and activity.)

Behavior Support Plan *(continued)*

6. Who is present/absent when the behavior occurs?

7. What is the reason for the behavior? What purpose does the behavior serve for the student? (for example, a sensory need, the desire to escape or avoid an activity or a person, a need for attention, or a desire for a tangible object.)

8. Identify alternate behaviors that could serve the same purpose.

9. Provide reinforcement strategies to support student learning, including verbal praise, desired tangible items, a choice of preferred item or activity, and free time.

10. Provide modifications and support in the school/classroom environment, such as verbal cues, preparing for transitions, picture schedules, choices, rewrite assignments to reduce unnecessary material on a page and/or to reduce the amount of questions or problems.

Behavior Support Plan

Date:

Name of student:

Review plan by:

1. Describe the behavior, including frequency.

2. What occurred directly before the behavior?

3. What occurred after the behavior?

4. When does the behavior occur? (For example, during transitional periods such as before and after activities, during particular activities)

5. Where does the behavior occur? (Give location and activity.)

Behavior Support Plan *(continued)*

6. Who is present/absent when the behavior occurs?

7. What is the reason for the behavior? What purpose does the behavior serve for the student? (for example, a sensory need, the desire to escape or avoid an activity or a person, a need for attention, or a desire for a tangible object.)

8. Identify alternate behaviors that could serve the same purpose.

9. Provide reinforcement strategies to support student learning, including verbal praise, desired tangible items, a choice of preferred item or activity, and free time.

10. Provide modifications and support in the school/classroom environment, such as verbal cues, preparing for transitions, picture schedules, choices, rewrite assignments to reduce unnecessary material on a page and/or to reduce the amount of questions or problems.

Behavior Support Plan

Date:

Name of student:

Review plan by:

1. Describe the behavior, including frequency.

2. What occurred directly before the behavior?

3. What occurred after the behavior?

4. When does the behavior occur? (For example, during transitional periods such as before and after activities, during particular activities)

5. Where does the behavior occur? (Give location and activity.)

6. Who is present/absent when the behavior occurs?

7. What is the reason for the behavior? What purpose does the behavior serve for the student? (for example, a sensory need, the desire to escape or avoid an activity or a person, a need for attention, or a desire for a tangible object.)

8. Identify alternate behaviors that could serve the same purpose.

9. Provide reinforcement strategies to support student learning, including verbal praise, desired tangible items, a choice of preferred item or activity, and free time.

10. Provide modifications and support in the school/classroom environment, such as verbal cues, preparing for transitions, picture schedules, choices, rewrite assignments to reduce unnecessary material on a page and/or to reduce the amount of questions or problems.

Behavior Support Plan

Date:

Name of student:

Review plan by:

1. Describe the behavior, including frequency.

2. What occurred directly before the behavior?

3. What occurred after the behavior?

4. When does the behavior occur? (For example, during transitional periods such as before and after activities, during particular activities)

5. Where does the behavior occur? (Give location and activity.)

Behavior Support Plan *(continued)*

6. Who is present/absent when the behavior occurs?

7. What is the reason for the behavior? What purpose does the behavior serve for the student? (for example, a sensory need, the desire to escape or avoid an activity or a person, a need for attention, or a desire for a tangible object.)

8. Identify alternate behaviors that could serve the same purpose.

9. Provide reinforcement strategies to support student learning, including verbal praise, desired tangible items, a choice of preferred item or activity, and free time.

10. Provide modifications and support in the school/classroom environment, such as verbal cues, preparing for transitions, picture schedules, choices, rewrite assignments to reduce unnecessary material on a page and/or to reduce the amount of questions or problems.

Behavior Support Plan

Date:

Name of student:

Review plan by:

1. Describe the behavior, including frequency.

2. What occurred directly before the behavior?

3. What occurred after the behavior?

4. When does the behavior occur? (For example, during transitional periods such as before and after activities, during particular activities)

5. Where does the behavior occur? (Give location and activity.)

6. Who is present/absent when the behavior occurs?

7. What is the reason for the behavior? What purpose does the behavior serve for the student? (for example, a sensory need, the desire to escape or avoid an activity or a person, a need for attention, or a desire for a tangible object.)

8. Identify alternate behaviors that could serve the same purpose.

9. Provide reinforcement strategies to support student learning, including verbal praise, desired tangible items, a choice of preferred item or activity, and free time.

10. Provide modifications and support in the school/classroom environment, such as verbal cues, preparing for transitions, picture schedules, choices, rewrite assignments to reduce unnecessary material on a page and/or to reduce the amount of questions or problems.

Behavior Support Plan

Date:

Name of student:

Review plan by:

1. Describe the behavior, including frequency.

2. What occurred directly before the behavior?

3. What occurred after the behavior?

4. When does the behavior occur? (For example, during transitional periods such as before and after activities, during particular activities)

5. Where does the behavior occur? (Give location and activity.)

6. Who is present/absent when the behavior occurs?

7. What is the reason for the behavior? What purpose does the behavior serve for the student? (for example, a sensory need, the desire to escape or avoid an activity or a person, a need for attention, or a desire for a tangible object.)

8. Identify alternate behaviors that could serve the same purpose.

9. Provide reinforcement strategies to support student learning, including verbal praise, desired tangible items, a choice of preferred item or activity, and free time.

10. Provide modifications and support in the school/classroom environment, such as verbal cues, preparing for transitions, picture schedules, choices, rewrite assignments to reduce unnecessary material on a page and/or to reduce the amount of questions or problems.

Index